WE THE PEOPLE

ESCAPING THE LAND OF DELUSION

By D.C. FULLER

ISBN:9798684516320
LCCN:2020917652

FOR THE SURVIVORS

AS WITH *'I THE PEOPLE'* YOU'LL FIND QUOTES, ARTICLES/EXCERPTS, AND LINKS TO ARTICLES THAT PERTAIN TO THE SUBJECT MATTER INSIDE. YOU'LL ALSO FIND MANY QUOTES FROM THE SCIENTIST/BIOLOGIST, RACHEL CARSON, ESPECIALLY FROM HER BOOK, *'SILENT SPRING'*, WHICH IS A COMPILATION OF ALL THE RESEARCH DONE ON THE CHEMICAL ASSAULT MANKIND HAS LEVELED AGAINST THE PLANET AND HIMSELF UP TO ITS PUBLISHING IN 1962. I STRONGLY SUGGEST YOU READ IT. YOU'LL ALSO FIND A GREAT MANY QUOTES FROM ONE OF THE GREATEST MINDS OF THE NINETEENTH CENTURY, FRIEDRICH NIETZSCHE. NIETZSCHE AND OTHER GREAT THINKERS THROUGHOUT THE AGE OF MAN SAW THE HANDWRITING ON THE WALL AND THOUGH THEY TRIED TO ARTICULATE THEIR VISION CLEARLY, WHAT WAS CLEAR TO THEM OFTEN ESCAPED THE SEMI-LITERATE MASSES, SO THEIR KNOWLEDGE WAS LOST TO ALL BUT THE FEW THAT SOUGHT THEM OUT. THE TRUTH AND KNOWLEDGE THEY IMPARTED IS AS VALUABLE TODAY, IF NOT MORE SO, THAN WHEN THEY WROTE IT, THEREFORE I FELT IT ONLY FITTING TO INCLUDE THE THOUGHTS AND WORDS OF SOME OF THE GREATEST MINDS THAT EVER EXISTED ON THE SUBJECTS IN THIS WORK. WITHOUT THEIR SHOULDERS TO STAND ON I FOR ONE WOULD NEVER HAVE EXISTED IN MY CURRENT CAPACITY.
D.C. FULLER

THE PAST IS THE BEST PREDICTOR OF THE FUTURE.

THE ONLY WAY WE'LL CHANGE ANYTHING IS BY CHANGING EVERYTHING.

"I AM A FIRM BELIEVER IN THE PEOPLE. IF GIVEN THE TRUTH, THEY CAN BE DEPENDED UPON TO MEET ANY NATIONAL CRISIS. THE GREAT POINT IS TO BRING THEM THE REAL FACTS." – Abraham Lincoln

"TURN OFF YOUR MIND RELAX AND FLOAT DOWNSTREAM,
IT IS NOT DYING.
LAY DOWN ALL THOUGHTS, SURRENDER TO THE VOID,
IT IS SHINING.
YET YOU MAY SEE THE MEANING OF WITHIN,
IT IS BEING.

THAT LOVE IS ALL AND LOVE IS EVERYONE,
IT IS KNOWING.
AND IGNORANCE AND HATE MAY MOURN THE DEAD,
IT IS BELIEVING.
BUT LISTEN TO THE COLOR OF YOUR DREAMS,
IT IS NOT LEAVING.
SO, PLAY THE GAME, 'EXISTENCE', TO THE END,
OF THE BEGINNING.
– *Tomorrow Never Knows*, John Lennon and Paul McCartney. The Beatles, *Revolver*

THE ELITE THAT CLAIM TO OWN THIS WORLD ARE NOTHING MORE THAN PARASITES THAT HAVE BAMBOOZLED YOU INTO BELIEVING THEY'RE POWERFUL WITH THE MOST WORTHLESS TRINKETS IMAGINABLE AND YOU'VE FALLEN FOR THEIR LIES HOOK LINE AND SINKER. ALL THE TRAUMA AND DRAMA THEY CREATE IS JUST A DISTRACTION SO YOU'LL NEVER FIGURE OUT HOW WEAK AND USELESS THEY REALLY ARE AND HOW POWERFUL WE ARE.

EVERYTHING YOU BELIEVE HAS POWER OVER YOU ONLY HAS IT BECAUSE YOU ALLOW IT. OVER MANY MILLENIA YOU'VE BEEN CONDITIONED AND MANIPULATED INTO BELIEVING THAT MONEY AND THOSE THAT POSSESS IT HAVE POWER, WHEN IN FACT, YOU'RE THE POWER AND THEY'RE THE WEAKEST OF ALL BECAUSE THEIR ONLY POWER IS LIES, MAKE-BELIEVE, AND WORTHLESS STRIPS OF PAPER. WITHOUT OUR POWER THEY'RE NOTHING.

"THE PEOPLE WHO ARE CRAZY ENOUGH TO THINK THEY CAN CHANGE THE WORLD ARE THE ONES WHO DO." – Rob Siltanen

"WE CANNOT SOLVE OUR PROBLEMS WITH THE SAME THINKING WE USED WHEN WE CREATED THEM." – Albert Einstein

INNOVATION AND PROGRESS ARE BORN OUT OF NECESSITY. AS I SEE IT, THERE'S NO GREATER NECESSITY THAN REVITALIZING OUR ENVIRONMENT AND ENDING HUMAN DEVOLUTION.

OBTAINING SOMETHING YOU'VE NEVER HAD REQUIRES DOING SOMETHING YOU'VE NEVER DONE. UNIFY, WE'LL DO IT TOGETHER.

<u>"YOU NEVER CHANGE THINGS BY FIGHTING THE EXISTING REALITY. TO CHANGE SOMETHING, BUILD A NEW MODEL THAT MAKES THE OLD MODEL OBSOLETE."</u> – R. Buckminster Fuller

"THE SECRET OF CHANGE IS TO FOCUS ALL OF YOUR ENERGY, NOT ON FIGHTING THE OLD, BUT ON BUILDING THE NEW." – Socrates

"DESPERATION IS THE RAW MATERIAL OF CHANGE. ONLY THOSE WHO CAN LEAVE BEHIND EVERYTHING THEY HAVE EVER BELIEVED IN CAN HOPE TO ESCAPE." – William S. Burroughs

"WE STAND NOW WHERE TWO ROADS DIVERGE, BUT UNLIKE THE ROADS IN ROBERT FROST'S FAMILIAR POEM, THEY ARE NOT EQUALLY FAIR. THE ROAD WE HAVE LONG BEEN TRAVELING IS DECEPTIVELY EASY, A SMOOTH SUPERHIGHWAY ON WHICH WE PROGRESS WITH GREAT SPEED, BUT AT ITS END LIES DISASTER. THE OTHER FORK OF THE ROAD – THE ONE LESS TRAVELED BY – OFFERS OUR LAST, OUR ONLY CHANCE TO REACH A DESTINATION THAT ASSURES THE PRESERVATION OF THE EARTH." – Rachel Carson, 'Silent Spring'

You're probably not gonna like much of this book, if you even finish it, because it's brutally honest and requires your education and taking responsibility for and drastically changing your thoughts and actions in order to make this plan to "save" this planet (the planet will be fine once it exterminates humanity) and in turn you, work.

Make no mistake, it won't be easy to undo all the damage the elite's greed has wrought on the planet and its citizens over the millennia and there'll be a lot of resistance from them and their minions to overcome before we can even begin. I often wonder if their resistance or yours will be the most difficult. You have thousands of years of conditioning to overcome before we even get to the point where the elite's resistance is an issue. I only hope you're up to it. If you are, it will take a lot of ingenuity and many years of steady and seemingly endless hard work just to reach the goals in this narrative. If not, you're letting humanity in for a world of unimagineable hurt simply because those in power care nothing about the destruction they're doing as long as they're making money.

I'm absolutely positive the powers-that-be and their alleged "experts" will deride it as impossible, deny its feasibility tooth and nail, and stick many disparaging labels on me, but I guarantee you I could care less about what anyone thinks because people don't think, they react the way they were conditioned to and it's the only plan that will.

Nonetheless, I urge you to think about, and remember this as you hear their derision and denial…those powers and experts are the people that brought humankind to this devolved state via a toxic environment degraded by greed, stupidity, and a myriad of environmental and societal stressors created by and for the sake of proliferating multiple forms of TRIBISM and its inherent violence.

In '*I THE PEOPLE*' I precisely named those powers but there's far too many "experts" to name. However, I can tell you how to identify them…they're the people in suits you see on the mainstream news allegedly explaining why things are happening and/or how they're gonna fix them. You can either keep reading and possibly break free of their deathgrip or continue listening to the people that have you bobsledding toward oblivion.

HUMANS HAVE A REMARKABLE CAPACITY FOR KINDNESS AND AN EVEN MORE REMARKABLE CAPACITY TO BE 100 TIMES MORE CRUEL THAN KIND.

"I AM PESSIMISTIC ABOUT THE HUMAN RACE BECAUSE IT IS TOO INGENIOUS FOR ITS OWN GOOD. OUR APPROACH TO NATURE IS TO BEAT IT INTO SUBMISSION. WE WOULD STAND A BETTER CHANCE OF SURVIVAL IF WE ACCOMMODATED OURSELVES TO THIS PLANET AND VIEWED IT APPRECIATIVELY INSTEAD OF SKEPTICALLY AND DICTATORIALLY." – E. B. White

WELCOME TO THE PEOPOCALYPSE. TAKE A NUMBER AND HAVE A SEAT. OVER 7.8 BILLION DISERVICED AND RISING.

"AND IS THAT NOT OUR FATE? WHAT TODAY CONSTITUTES *OUR* ANTIPATHY TO "MAN"? – FOR WE *SUFFER* FROM MAN, BEYOND DOUBT." – Friedrich Nietzsche, *On the Genealogy of Morals*

"THE SIGHT OF MAN NOW MAKES US WEARY – WHAT IS NIHILISM TODAY IF IT IS NOT *THAT*? – WE ARE WEARY OF *MAN*." – Friedrich Nietzsche, *On the Genealogy of Morals*

I KILL YOU!

"THE QUESTION IS WHETHER ANY CIVILIZATION CAN WAGE A RELENTLESS WAR ON LIFE WITHOUT DESTROYING ITSELF, AND WITHOUT LOSING THE RIGHT TO BE CALLED CIVILIZED." – Rachel Carson

THE PERFECT STORM

"WHY SHOULD WE TOLERATE A DIET OF WEAK POISONS, A HOME OF INSIPID SURROUNDINGS, A CIRCLE OF ACQUAINTANCES WHO ARE NOT QUITE OUR ENEMIES, THE NOISE OF MOTORS WITH JUST ENOUGH RELIEF TO PREVENT INSANITY? WHO WOULD WANT TO LIVE IN A WORLD WHICH IS JUST NOT QUITE FATAL?" – Paul Shepard, from Rachel Carson's, '*Silent Spring*'

"HE WHO BY MEANS OF HIS KNOWLEDGE PLUNGES NATURE INTO THE ABYSS OF DESTRUCTION MUST ALSO SUFFER THE DISSOLUTION OF NATURE IN HIS OWN PERSON." – Freidrich Nietzsche, *The Birth of Tragedy*

I published '*I THE PEOPLE*' in August of 2018. I almost wrote these two books simultaineously. I had every intention of publishing this book soon after publishing ITP, but once I published ITP it seemed like the wind in my sails died and I had no desire to continue with *'WE THE PEOPLE'*, which at that time was just the plan for reversing climate change and the devolution of humanity. Numerous times throughout the following year I picked up my computer to put the finishing touches on WTP but only ended up staring at it with a completely blank mind for a few hours and putting it away.

However, as a Socio-Psychological Anthropologist I continued to watch humanity's decline as closely as I ever did during my fifty years of participant-observation, as well as listen to the "experts" often ridiculous explanations. I even reached out to numerous news agencies in an attempt to set the record straight in hopes that it may help humanity right its course only to find that mainstream news was only concerned with presenting the Hegelian Dialectic of escalating problems, emotional reactions, and ridiculous "solutions" from politicians' alleged "experts" with lots of intials behind their names but little else.

On the 211th day of 2019, America had its 249th mass shooting at a Walmart in El Paso, Texas. As usual, socialists were quick to blame Trump's anti-migrant rhetoric because Patrick Crusius told authorities he did it to kill the Mexicans he claimed were invading his country.

Thirteen hours later, one hour into the 212th day of 2019, Connor Betts, killed his own sister while committing the 250th mass shooting in the Oregon District of Dayton, Ohio, which is essentially my backyard, allegedly due to his alignment with ANTIFA.

Between August 4th and August 31st, When Seth Ator committed the 251st mass shooting in Odessa, Texas, the FBI claims to have thwarted seventeen other mass shootings around the country and the "experts" claimed the shootings could be attributed to the gunmens' desire for "power and control," which couldn't be further from the truth. No one mentioned the 141 individual shootings that happened in the first week after the Dayton shooting though. What do you think the motives were for those?

As with everything Americans don't like, groups all over the country got their magic markers, cardboard, and sticks together, made signs and marched around screaming "DO SOMETHING!" while socialists blamed Trump and guns, Trump blamed mental illness and inadequate background checks, and the "experts" gave press conferences blaming lots of things. None of which made much sense, except a smidgen of the mental illness excuse, but we're gonna get a lot deeper into that very soon.

Blaming Trump's anti-migrant rhetoric is ridiculous. I heard the same rhetoric and thought he was an idiot. It was JFK's policies that created the problems in Central America in the first place and those chickens had to come home to roost some time, especially after the socialists took over.

Blaming guns for shootings is like blaming spoons for obesity. And, if the "experts" are so expert why are there any shootings at all, let alone mass shootings? Maybe their expertise lays elsewhere? Maybe they're deeply indocrinated fools giving lip-service to an issue they really know nothing about. Or, could it be they know exactly why and are lying to us?

It's worth noting that while the U.S. is experiencing a rising tide of gun crime and mass shootings, gunless countries are being inundated with suicide bombings, gang rapes, mass stabbings, acid attacks, mass vehicular assaults, cultural assassinations, economic catastrophes, car bombings, the destruction of entire segments of cities, and the overwhelming of their legal and welfare systems. The leaders of these countries that accused Trump of Islamophobia and Xenophobia when he attempted to ban Muslim immigrants and immigrants in general in 2017 have quietly closed their borders and are beginning to deport immigrants for multiple reasons. Gross hypocricy isn't confined to American politicians, it's the stock in trade of all governments and politicians everywhere.

Now let's get down to the real cause(s):

BETTER LIVING THROUGH CHEMISTRY
"THE SCIENCES, EACH STRAINING IN ITS OWN DIRECTION, HAVE
HITHERTO HARMED US LITTLE; BUT SOME DAY THE PIECING

TOGETHER OF DISSOCIATED KNOWLEDGE WILL OPEN UP SUCH TERRIFYING VISTAS OF REALITY, AND OF OUR FRIGHTFUL POSITION THEREIN, THAT WE SHALL EITHER GO MAD FROM THE REVELATION OR FLEE FROM THE DEADLY LIGHT INTO THE PEACE AND SAFETY OF A NEW DARK AGE." – H.P. Lovecraft

"A WHO'S WHO OF PESTICIDES IS THEREFORE A CONCERN TO US ALL. IF WE ARE GOING TO LIVE SO INTIMATELY WITH THESE CHEMICALS EATING AND DRINKING THEM, TAKING THEM INTO THE VERY MARROW OF OUR BONES – WE HAD BETTER KNOW SOMETHING ABOUT THEIR NATURE AND POWER." – Rachel Carson, *'Silent Spring'*

About 4500 years ago the first pesticide, elemental sulfur dust, was used on crops by the Sumerians in Mesopotamia and was eventually one of the many natural pesticides used from the Hellispont to the Indus Valley at the height of Persian culture, with Pyrethrum (Persian Powder, a treatment for lice), made from Crysanthemums, being the most prevalent. However, it really wasn't until Paul Muller discovered DDT in 1939 that pesticide use became as prolific, and toxic, as it is now.

Among a growing list of organic and inorganically based pesticides DDT seemed to be a dream come true. It worked on a wide range of pests and was allegedly innocuous to humans. When I was a kid we used to ride our bicycles in the DDT fog emitted by the "mosquito truck" when it came around a couple times a summer. The scientist, Rachel Carson, sounded the alarm about the toxicity of DDT and the cornicopia of even more toxic pesticides and herbicides in use in her book '*SILENT SPRING*' in 1962, which led to DDT finally being banned in 1972, not so much because of '*SILENT SPRING*' and the toxicity but because insects had become resistant to it.

"MANY CHEMICALS USED AS PESTICIDES – HERBICIDES AS WELL AS INSECTICIDES – BELONG TO THIS GROUP OF SUBSTANCES THAT HAVE THE ABILITY TO DAMAGE CHROMOSOMES, INTERFERE WITH NORMAL CELL DIVISION, OR CAUSE MUTATIONS. THESE INJURIES TO THE GENETIC MATERIAL ARE OF A KIND THAT MAY LEAD TO DISEASE IN THE INDIVIDUAL EXPOSED OR THEY MAY MAKE THEIR EFFECTS FELT IN FUTURE GENERATIONS." – Rachel Carson, '*Silent Spring*'

As DDT was being phased out the next broad spectrum pesticide, glyphosate, was being introduced, and, although a myriad of other inorganically based pesticides similar to glyphosate, with narrower effective ranges, were introduced as well, it was glyphosate that became the most popular.

Why am I telling you this? Because all pesticides are neurotoxins and/or carcinogens. It was also discovered that they don't break down over time, distance, or depth in the ground (1800 foot deep core samples found glyphosate unaltered); they've accumulated in our air, soil, water, plant and animal life, and food, and they're accumulating in our fatty tissues right now, which is essentially what our brains are made of and even though they may not seem to cause immediate problems, you'll see they've caused many problems down the road as you read on.

"ALL THIS HAS COME ABOUT BECAUSE OF THE SUDDEN RISE AND PRODIGIOUS GROWTH OF AN INDUSTRY FOR THE PRODUCTION OF MAN-MADE OR SYNTHETIC CHEMICALS WITH INSECTICIDAL PROPERTIES. THIS INDUSTRY IS A CHILD OF THE SECOND WORLD WAR. IN THE COURSE OF DEVELOPING AGENTS OF CHEMICAL WARFARE, SOME OF THE CHEMICALS CREATED IN THE LABORATORY WERE FOUND TO BE LETHAL TO INSECTS. THE DISCOVERY DID NOT COME BY CHANCE: INSECTS WERE WIDELY USED TO TEST CHEMICALS AS AGENTS OF DEATH FOR MAN." – Rachel Carson, '*Silent Spring*'

From as early as 1500 B.C. Egypt, man has been enhancing his food with artificial colorings and preservatives but it wasn't until the 1800's that regulation became a priority. Up until then people regularly ingested a myriad of poisonous chemicals and minerals such as arsenic, copper, chromium, lead, mercury, zinc, bituminous coal, and many many more heavy metals, inorganic elements, and toxic dyes that were used to extend the life of and add pleasing colors to our foods. This resulted in thousands of illnesses and deaths over time and was finally addressed in Germany in 1882.

The Irish custom of a "Wake" before a burial came about as a result of a toxicity that mimicked death from drinking large amounts of alcohol out of lead vessels and tankards. The "death" that resulted lasted anywhere from a few hours to four or five days. During that time the "dead's" heartbeat and respiration all but stopped giving them the appearance of being dead until the toxic shock wore off and they woke up, often in a coffin underground.

The Irish decided it would be a good idea to have a party celebrating the deceased that lasted four or five days to give the "dead" time to wake up instead of prematurely burying a friend or relative. The custom spread rather quickly as premature burials became very common during the industrialization of Europe. Due to the citizenry's constant exposure to toxic chemicals and premature "deaths," coffins were fitted with a hole in the top a string passed through that was tied to a bell above ground and the hand of the deceased so the bell would ring if they awoke after burial and began thrashing around. The term "graveyard shift" originated with the job of monitoring graveyards for ringing bells overnight.

The 'Pure Food and Drug Act of 1906' reduced the number of acceptable additives from 700 to seven in the United States but that list has grown considerably since then with the advent of synthetic additives and an ever more corrupt government owned by the elite's corporations. Although it was passed in 1906 it took decades to rid foods of the toxic chemicals due to the bought-off politicians owned by the food industry confounding and blocking the enforcement of the bill at every turn.

Upton Sinclair's book, *THE JUNGLE* (1906), was written about the corruption of the Chicago meat packing industry at the turn of the twentieth century. It chronicled the highly toxic environment of, The Back of the Yards, the impoverished neighborhood adjacent to the slaughterhouses where the employees of the packing plants lived and died due to the dangers and poisons in the workplace, the food, the water, the air, and the squalid conditions the meat barons forced them to endure just to have a job that only paid pennys per day.

As a child I was frenetic (hyperactivity caused by artificial colorings and/or flavorings) due to my love of ketchup on everything, Hawaiian Punch and Jordan's (red) Natural Casing Hotdogs, which were loaded with Red Dye #3.

The ketchup on my eggs at breakfast got me going, nonetheless, I was still somewhat manageable during the first half of a school day. However, once I went home for lunch and had a couple red hotdogs and glasses of Hawaiian Punch I was impossible to handle and drove my teachers crazy. I wouldn't shut up, sit still, or stop bothering all the other students around me, which usually resulted in a beating with the blackboard pointer, an inch square yardstick, or 'The Board of Education' and spending the rest of the afternoon standing in a corner in the hallway. This continued until 1966 when Red Dye #3 was finally banned.

IF YOU WANNA FEEL HAPPY, TAKE A PILL!!

As the chemical onslaught on and in our environment and food escalated so did the chemical onslaught on our bodies and brains escalate with pharmaceuticals. There's now a pill for everything and the vast majority of them cause more problems than they cure. Does it really make sense to take something for a medical malady that has a list of adverse side-effects longer than your arm or a greater possibility of killing you than the original issue? The "medical/pharmaceutical professionals" seem to think so and unless you do your due diligence on everything you're prescribed you're putting your life in the hands of pill pushing profiteers that only care about money, as evidenced by the current opioid crisis and the myriad problems ninety-nine percent of prescription drugs cause. For which, of course, they have ever more pills.

When researching the vast majority of pharmaceuticals available today it's impossible not to arrive at the realization that they're mostly neurotoxins, especially the pyschiatric drugs. Dr. Peter Breggin, a Harvard-trained psychiatrist and best selling author, has spent his entire career trying to expose and curb the propensity of his profession to push pills on its patients, with little success, as even the F.D.A. is against him.

Today, a child such as myself would be medicated six ways from Sunday in order to get them to conform to classroom decorum. And, it isn't just pyschiatric drugs that are dangerous, it's seemingly innocuous drugs like COPD inhalers or talcum powder that no one would suspect. If you review the side effects listed in the product insert of nearly any drug you're prescribed you'll find a long list of side effects with some minor and major neurological issues, including death, listed. You'll have to do a little more research to find the really horrendous ones, but you'll be glad you did. It could save you some serious problems down the road.

Don't think you're safe if you're not using pharmaceuticals though. Studies have found there are quantities of every drug prescribed in our water systems, including what we think are pristine lakes and streams. You're probably doubting this can happen but how it happens is very simple.

People take their prescribed medications, those meds enter the water system when people urinate and deficate a few hours later. As well as when they dispose of unused meds by dumping them down the toilet. Waste treatment plants don't screen them out so they pass into the "clean" water those systems expel into the environment, which ends up in aquifers, lakes, streams, and reservoirs that supply water for drinking, irrigation, bathing, and recreation. Everything that comes in contact with that water injests those drugs one way or another, resulting in a society that's being bombarded with a multitude of drugs in their food, drink, and leaching through their integumentary system. Numerous books have been written about the subject recently, I suggest you avail yourself of the information.

THE NATURAL GAS SCAM

Touted by the greedy idiots in government as "the clean alternative to fossil fuels," natural gas is the exact opposite. The fracking industry has readily acknowledged that 594 of the 900 chemicals used in every fracking well around the world is a known neurotoxin or carcinogen but they still insist fracking isn't the cause of the problems found in the environment and populations around their wells despite mountains of evidence to the contrary (if it's so safe why do the CEOs of fracking companies insist that it doesn't take place within 100 miles of their homes?).

The truth is, the on-site containment tanks leak these toxins into the atmosphere daily and evaporation is used to keep the holding ponds of waste water at the drill sites from overflowing. The toxic dirty water in these ponds is sprayed into the air so the sun will evaporate it, which loads the atmosphere with neurotoxins and carcinogens that are then blown all around the world on the prevailing winds. It's also injected into the water table to get rid of it, which means it eventually ends up in reservoirs, aquifers, lakes, and streams. And, since fracking takes place all around the world now it's not difficult to understand why roughly thirty-five percent of the pollutants in our air come from fracking and over ninety percent, and climbing, of the water on this planet is unusable.

CHEMICAL SKIES

Intentional geoengineering began in the U.S. in 1891 with rainmaking, but the reality is that geoengineering began with the intentional felling of the first tree and the first man-made fire. Those simple acts that are hailed as the intellectual progress of man's evolution are responsible for the growing deserts around the world. The historical and archaeological records and simple common sense indicate that the North African and Middle Eastern areas that are now barren deserts were once lush forests and verdent savanas until man began his migrations out of Africa and spread around the globe.

The archaeological record indicates that man migrated with the animals as he hunted them out while hunting for food. The historical and archaeological records indicate that man became more sedentary and sophisticated when he invented agriculture, animal husbandry, and created cities to house the populations that worked the large agricultural areas, clearing the forests for building materials, fuel, grazing, and farmland. Common sense dictates that if these areas were deserts when man began migrating he would've never gotten beyond the Sahara Desert because there wouldn't have been any food or water to sustain him or the animals he was following.

As man deforested and desertified areas he settled, he simply picked up and moved on to greener pastures once an area became sterile. This pattern continues today resulting in the deforestation of over eighty percent of the planet with that number rising exponentially every day thanks to idiots like Xi, Trump, and Bolsonaro, as well as every other "leader" people think they've elected that values worthless strips of paper over the environment that sustains all life, which is all of them.

As a result of man's relentless destruction of the environment and the resulting drying of the atmosphere and decreased rains, actual geoengineering came into being in the late 1800s in an attempt to stave off the wind errosion of denuded earth/farmland and maintain and/or increase productivity levels of said farmland. The first efforts were simply the injection of massive amounts of particulates into the atmosphere with cannons and large fires because people noticed that rain usually followed large battles and forest fires.

When this had little to no success, chemical concoctions were boiled and allowed to evaporate into the atmosphere. For whatever reason this was successful for some rainmakers, too much so for several of them. A full blow by blow account of this is provided in the 'Rainmakers' section of '*I THE PEOPLE*'.

With the advent of aircraft, geoengineering took to the skies and a myriad of toxic chemicals and particulates, including soot, were sprayed from aircraft in what came to be known as "chemtrails" by the current "ecologist" counter-culture. The following is a list of the chemicals used. Pay close attention to the known affects they have on humans and see if you recognize those affects in the stories of escalating violence, abhorrent behaviors, mental and physical illnesses, birth defects, and societal devolution around the globe that dominates today's news.

The following are regularly purchased by geoengineering companies around the world and the many recipes for their chemical cocktails generally consist of several (usually five) of these ingredients at once, but never all of them, at least not that I've found.

Aluminum oxide particles = high concentrations found in the brains of Alzheimer patients, possible link to Autism

Arsenic = naturally occurring, but also used in rat poison, linked to lung, skin, kidney, and liver cancers

Bacilli and molds = staph and strep the most common, molds inhibit immune system function

Barium chloride = also in rat poison, toxic to humans, gastrointestinal

effects in young and cardiovascular in elderly, immunosuppression noted
Barium titanates = insulator that's polarizable with an electrical field, light refractor = respiratory and sinus issues
Cadmium nitrate = absorbs moisture from air, inhalation hazard – causes flu-like illness (metal fume fever), prolonged high dose exposure = pulmonary edema; prolonged low dose exposure = liver and kidney damage, anemia, loss of sense of smell
Calcium nitrate = absorbs moisture from the air, fertilizer, saltpeter
Hexavalent chromium = a carcinogen that invades the nuclei of cells causing breaks in DNA strands
Desiccated human red blood cells = removes the oxygen from surrounding viable red blood cells
Ethylene dibromide = the "lead" found harmful and removed from American gasoline in the 70s, carcinogen used in pesticides, 100% cancer causing to lungs, heart, liver
Enterobacter cloacae = nosocomial pathogens that cause lower respiratory, skin and soft tissue, urinary tract, intra-abdominal, septic arthritis, osteomyelitis, and ophthalmic infections
Enterobacteriaceae = a large bacterial family including salmonella and E. Coli
Human white blood cells = restrictor enzyme used in research labs to snip and combine DNA
Lead = known to cause 10% of intellectual disabilities and many behavioral problems, acute effects are seizures, coma, and death
Mercury = causes muscle weakness, poor coordination, numbness in extremities, kidney problems, decreased intelligence, and eventual insanity. The euphemism "mad as a hatter" was created to describe the effects the mercury in the glue used had on hat makers
Methyl aluminum = can cause respiratory distress, burning skin and eyes, and ignites and reignites spontaneously when mixed with air, producing poisonous fumes. Highly caustic and toxic when mixed with water
Mold spores = reactions include from cold symptoms to death depending on specie and amount
Mycoplasma = found to invade cell nuclei causing endocrine disruption and sex related birth defects, hermaphrodism being the most common
Nano-aluminum-coated fiberglass (CHAFF) = linked with emotional instability, poor impulse control, paranoia, uncontrollable rage, violent mood swings, delusional thoughts, and irrational behavior
Nitrogen trifluoride = a component of rocket fuels, highly toxic, highly volatile, causes respiratory distress and burns skin. Is an extreme fire

hazard and etches glass when moistened. Reacts violently to hydrogen, ammonia, carbon monoxide, methane, and charcoal

Nickel = though occurring naturally, nickel can cause respiratory problems in large amounts over time

Polymer fibers = inhalation hazard. Also found in Morgellons Disease lesions

Pseudomonas aeruginosa = a multi-drug resistant bacteria recognized for its ubiquity (appearing everywhere), intrinsically advanced antibiotic resistance mechanisms, and association with serious illness – hospital acquired infections, pneumonia, and sepsis

Pseudomonas florescens = innocuous except for those with compromised immune systems

Radioactive cesium = known for cell damage and cancer causation, may cause nausea, vomiting, coma, and death

Radioactive thorium = as used here is linked to cancer of the lungs, pancreas, and blood and liver disease

Selenium = present in the food chain

Serratia marcescens = an antibiotic resistant bacteria that's known to cause urinary tract infections and pneumonia

Sharp titanium shards = become embedded in mucus membranes and lung tissue compromising the viability of the tissue for oxygen transfer by creating scar tissue

Silver = a reflector or refractor

Streptomyces = antibiotic producing bacteria, but also used as an introduction or bonding agent due to its cell piercing properties

Strontium = heavy contributor to bone cancer and leukemia incidence

Sub-micron particles = (containing live biological matter)

Unidentified bacteria = superbacterias that have yet to be categorized or published

Uranium = absorbed strictly through respiration, accumulates in bone tissue, effects kidney, brain, and liver functions, has adverse effects on reproduction

Yellow fungal mycotoxins = toxic chemicals produced by yellow fungi that weaken a host's immunity to fungal infection

It should be noted that full air suits are required by OSHA for handling all of the previous items.

Again, the average chemtrail only contains a few of the above ingredients, (most often barium chloride and titanates, multiple bacterium, aluminum oxide, synthetic polymers [fibers], CHAFF, and ethylene dibromide), and that the variations are region and outcome specific. For the full story please refer to the 'Rainmakers' section of '*I THE PEOPLE*'.

Coincidentally, since the publication of '*I THE PEOPLE*' I've noticed chemtrailing has slowed considerably, at least in my part of the sky. I doubt very much it has anything to do with ITP though. It probably has more to do with its ineffectiveness, off the charts rising air pollution and ocean acidification, and the alleged shuttering of HAARP.

I first witnessed chemtrail activity while living in Los Angeles in 1988, which makes it safe to say that for the past 32 years things on the previous list of chemicals and particulates have been sprayed into the atmosphere with great regularity, making the air, water, and soil toxic. Combine this with pollution from fracking and oil wells, industry, automobiles, national and international commerce, pesticides and herbicides, and pharmaceuticals being disposed of in our sewer systems and we've created a perfect storm of toxic chemicals that continually poison our air, food, and water. However, I'm far from finished. This is actually just the beginning of the causes of the escalating violence, read on.

LIFELONG EXPOSURE TO AIR POLLUTION LINKED TO HIGHER RISK OF ALZHEIMERS

AFP Relax news.

This article's in toto: http://technology.inquirer.net/74967/lifelong-exposure-to-air-pollution-linked-to-higher-risk-of-alzheimers

April 17th 2018

New United States research has found that growing up in a city with a high level of air pollution could increase the risk of Alzheimer's disease and progression of the disease. Carried out by researchers at the University of Montana, the study looked at the effects of air pollution in Mexico City, where 24 million people in the metropolitan area are exposed daily to concentrations of fine particulate matter (PM2.5) and ozone pollution above U.S. Environmental Protection Agency standards.

The team looked at 203 autopsies of Mexico City residents, who ranged in age from 11 months to 40 years, to measure the levels of two abnormal proteins which indicate the development of Alzheimer's: hyperphosphorylated tau and beta amyloid. The results showed that 99.5 percent of the subjects examined showed signs of Alzheimer's disease, with the early stages of the disease even found in babies less than a year old. The young adult city dwellers, who had had a lifetime of exposure to PM2.5, also showed high levels of both proteins in the brain.

In addition to the proteins tau and amyloid, the team also looked at the gene apolipoprotein E (APOE 4), which is a well-known risk factor

for Alzheimer's. This time the team found that not only was the progression of Alzheimer's related to age and PM2.5 exposure, but it was also linked with APOE 4, with APOE 4 carriers showing a higher risk of rapid progression of the disease as well as 4.92 higher odds of committing suicide compared to those who don't carry the gene.

The team concluded that exposure to PM2.5 had a negative effect on the progression of the disease due to the tiny pollution particles entering the brain through the nose, lungs and gastrointestinal tract from where they can travel everywhere in the body through the circulatory system causing damage. They added in their conclusion that air pollution is one of the key modifiable risk for millions of people across the world, including millions of Americans exposed to harmful particulate pollution levels. "Alzheimer's disease hallmarks start in childhood in polluted environments, and we must implement effective preventative measures early," said lead researchers Dr. Lilian Calderón-Garcidueñas. "It is useless to take reactive actions decades later. Neuroprotection measures ought to start very early, including the prenatal period and childhood. Defining pediatric environmental, nutritional, metabolic and genetic risk-factor interactions are key to preventing Alzheimer's disease."

The results can be found published online in the journal of Environmental Research. JB

VACCINES

Despite the government's constant assertion that vaccines are safe it's paid out over $4.5billion in compensation for the damages vaccines have caused. There's actually a laundry list of possible/probable damages vaccines are capable of causing depending on the prior genetic mutations of the parents and the current genetic mutations of the vaccinated, immune system strength or lack thereof, exposure to environmental contaminants, and the numerous toxic contents in the vaccines.

The experts are constantly expounding on the need of a Covid-19 vaccine before it can be contained, often citing the Spanish Flu pandemic and Polio as proof of their accersion, but there was no vaccine for the Spanish Flu. Ultimately, it was improved personal hygiene and public sanitation that slowed it down, with isolation and quarantining giving those measures time to become effective. Almost the same thing goes for Polio with the exception that there was a vaccine for Polio, however its true efficacy is questionable due to the concurrent large-scale implementation of public sanitation.

I'm going to leave it at that because to thoroughly cover the subject would require the writing of another book and there's already several of those. It's sufficient to say that vaccines have a deleterious affect on society's health (physical and mental) by weakening, occasionally destroying, one's immune system (anti-bacterial soaps and sanitizers also weaken the immune system), which has an impact on the escalating violence in the world by making people more susceptible to the effects of neurotoxins, as well as carcinogens. Of course that will be vehemently denied by the "experts," whose only expertise is upholding the lies of the elite.

RADIATION
"IN ONE OF THE MORE UNPLEASANT PORTENTS OF THE TIMES, THE OFFICE OF VITAL STATISTICS IN 1961 INITIATED A NATIONAL TABULATION OF MALFORMATIONS AT BIRTH, WITH THE EXPLANATORY COMMENT THAT THE RESULTING STATISTICS WOULD PROVIDE NEEDED FACTS ON THE INCIDENCE OF CONGENITAL MALFORMATIONS AND THE CIRCUMSTANCES UNDER WHICH THEY OCCUR. SUCH STUDIES WILL NO DOUBT BE DIRECTED LARGELY TOWARD MEASURING THE EFFECTS OF RADIATION, BUT IT MUST NOT BE OVERLOOKED THAT MANY CHEMICALS ARE THE PARTNERS OF RADIATION, PRODUCING PRECISELY THE SAME EFFECTS." – Rachel Carson, '*Silent Spring*'

As with the vaccines, the affects of microwave bombardment/radiation would require another book to fully cover and there are already plenty of them out there. Suffice it to say that the radiation from the numerous sources of microwaves/radiation (cell phones/towers, satellite television/internet, wifi, computers, smart grids/systems, microwave ovens, etc.) we're exposed to daily have a deleterious affect on every cell in our bodies as well as everything we ingest.

Microwave weapons perfected by DARPA are used by our government. Many of which were tested and perfected during Desert Storm. The military used a 1 millimeter broadband (5G) 'Voice of God' microwave weapon created by DARPA against the Iraqi troops that caused several hundred of them to lay down their weapons and surrender because they claimed to have heard the voice of god in their heads telling them to do so. Now they intend to use that same technology for the next generation 5G cell phone network and what else only the elite know for sure, but if China's use of it is any indication, it's not good.

The short wavelength broadband system will require towers to be erected every 300 yards in urban and suburban areas in order to provide a seamless blanket of microwave coverage. In essense, urban and suburbanites will be living in a microwave oven 24/7/365. It's claimed this will enhance cellphone services, making them exponentially more convenient, but for who? By the time we find out it'll be too late to do anything about it.

China already has its 5G system in operation. There are 200 million surveillance cameras, 783 million smart phones, and 960 million IoT devices in use across China. Its citizens are under survellience every second, resulting in over 13 million of them being blacklisted already. Most of them have been rounded up and interned in "re-education camps" to be brainwashed into State compliance. Chinese movie star, Fan Bingbing, was recently renditioned and re-educated because The Party/State felt her stardom in an American movie elevated her above it and she had to be "put in her place." Chairman Xi thinks this would be good for everyone around the world and Trump agrees.

No one knows for certain what the outcome of combining radiation and the toxic chemical cocktail we're exposed to daily can possibly be for every individual due to a multitude of variables, but many scientists have been working on it since the `50's and have many theories; given the current increasingly volatile violence prone society that's constantly devolving I would say many of them are right on track.

"THE LIVING CELL ASSAULTED BY RADIATION SUFFERS A VARIETY OF INJURIES: ITS ABILITY TO DIVIDE NORMALLY MAY BE DESTROYED, IT MAY SUFFER CHANGES IN CHROMOSOME STRUCTURE, OR THE GENES, CARRIERS OF HEREDITARY MATERIAL, MAY UNDERGO THOSE SUDDEN CHANGES KNOWN AS MUTATIONS, WHICH CAUSE THEM TO PRODUCE NEW CHARACTERISTICS IN SUCCEEDING GENERATIONS. IF ESPECIALLY SUSCEPTIBLE THE CELL MAY BE KILLED OUTRIGHT, OR FINALLY, AFTER THE PASSAGE OF TIME MEASURED IN YEARS, IT MAY BECOME MALIGNANT." – Rachel Carson, 'Silent Spring'

"THE GROWING EXPOSURE OF THE POPULATION TO RADIATION FROM VARIOUS SOURCES, PLUS THE MANY CONTACTS WITH A HOST OF CHEMICALS SUGGEST A GRAVE NEW PROBLEM FOR THE MODERN WORLD." – Rachel Carson, 'Silent Spring'

THE CODDLING OF THE AMERICAN MIND
"WORDS HURT"
Words and images only have the power you allow them. If your feelings are hurt by words, icons, or images, it's your problem, not the speaker's, artist's, or maker's. Having hurt feelings or being

offended doesn't prove you're right, it proves you're thoroughly ensconced in learned fragility and learned helplessness.

"Sticks and stones will break my bones but words will never hurt me. I know you are but what am I? I'm rubber, you're glue, what you say bounces off me and sticks to you!" Those are just a few of the retorts used when called a name, teased, picked on, or given a hard time about something by acquaintances, strangers, or enemies when I was growing up. As children of "the greatest generation" we were expected to stand our ground on our own two feet, fight our own battles, and not give a damn what others thought of us, or said about or to us.

If your little battle of words got physical you were expected to give back everything you got, silence your tormentor, and make them regret choosing you to pick on. Once the scuffle was over you went your own ways, or as often happened to me, you became friends. I met every friend I had growing up in a fight. We created our own unshakeable concept of self that couldn't even be scratched by my high school English teacher, Ma Leary's, assessment that I was, "a slimey little thing that crawled out from under a rock and deserved to be smushed like one" for talking during detention, or my dad's constant barrage of insults every time we interacted.

The job of every parent is to prepare their children to become successful independent adults, not to be their friend. To that end my father used the then traditional, "children should be beaten and not heard" method. He ignored me unless I interrupted his newspaper reading, his TV watching, or got into trouble my mother didn't want to handle. In any case his solution was a beating and a shouting of the epithet, "this kid's gonna be dead or in prison by the time he's sixteen, and if he's dead I hope I'm the one that killed him!!" when it was over. My mother's method was a little gentler. She asked once, told twice, and blistered me with the belt if I had to be told a third time. My dad did the same thing on the infrequent occasion he told me to do something. The rules were laid out for me early on and beat into my backside with a belt or whatever else was handy whenever I forgot them.

I was taught financial independence and the difference between want and need with one word, "no," and three sentences, "you don't need that," "we can't afford that," and/or "when you have your own money you can buy whatever you want." With that in mind I joined the work force as soon as I was able. I mowed lawns, did yard work, shoveled snow, and worked as a laborer/assistant to a few neighborhood handymen. My parents provided what I needed, except at birthdays and

Christmas when I ususally got what I asked for, and I provided what I wanted as the fruits of my labors allowed the rest of the time.

At the end of WWII Russia rightly reasoned that American involvement was the turning point in the war. Up until that time, the Axis powers, Nazi Germany and Japan, were steamrolling over all their targets and seemed unstoppable. In the Russian government's eyes America looked like the next big threat to the worldwide domination of communism because it was our involvement that turned the tide. They reasoned their next big enemy, America, was strong due to the overall strength of individual Americans and decided to initiate a KGB plan that would weaken Americans psychologically over time called 'Ideological Subversion', which was outlined in 1984 by KGB defector, Yuri Alexandrovich Bezmenov, who defected to Canada in 1970, in an interview with G. Edward Griffin.

Bezmenov defined Ideological Subversion as "a great brainwashing process. What it basically means is: to change the perception of reality of every American to such an extent that despite the abundance of information no one is able to come to sensible conclusions in the interest of defending themselves, their families, their community, and their country." This brainwashing has four stages and takes generations to achieve as it initially requires a re-education of a generation of students to subvert western values with socialist values. This "contamination" of Marxist values began with the baby-boomers and the hippy movement in the late fifties and early sixties (evidenced by the socialist movements like the S.D.S. [Students for a Democratic Society] that permeated college campuses in the `50's and `60's) and entered government, civil service, business, mass media, and education in the `70's and `80's when baby-boomers entered those spheres.

The first stage, "demoralization," takes about fifteen to twenty years because it requires a re-education of students throughout their entire school life from kindergarten through college. Bezmenov describes demoralization thusly: "They are programmed to think and react to certain stimuli in a certain pattern. You cannot change their mind even if you expose them to authentic information. Even if you prove that white is white and black is black, you still cannot change the basic perception and the logic of behavior." He claims, once accomplished, demoralization is irreversible and that the gradually demoralized have no clue that it's happened.

Bezmenov describes a demoralized person thusly: "As I mentioned before, exposure to true information does not matter anymore. A person who was demoralized is unable to assess true information. The facts tell nothing to him. Even if I shower him with information, with authentic proof, with documents, with pictures; even if I take him by force to the Soviet Union and show him concentration camp, he will refuse to believe it, until he receives a kick in his fat bottom. When a military boot crashes his balls then he will understand. But not before that. That's the tragic situation of demoralization." Bezmenov states that the demoralization of America succeeded far beyond the expectations of its creators due to the extreme division between the myriad of social factions that reject facts and common sense in favor of lies, circular hollow rhetoric, idiotic opinions, baseless beliefs, and superstitions.

The next stage is "destabilization," a two to five-year process in which the subverter no longer cares about ideas or patterns; economy, foreign relations, and defense systems are all that matters, things in which Marxist-Leninist ideas have very evidently taken hold in America, evidenced by the rise of democratic socialists in government.

The next stage, "crisis," sets the hook. It only requires six weeks of crisis such as those in Central America during the socialist revolutions to bring about "a violent change of power, structure, and economy."

The final stage is "normalization," which is when the ideological changes become a false reality of fanciful trinkets, an unstable economy, and an allegedly benevolent big brother government that claims to have everything under control when the exact opposite is true. "If people will fail to grasp the impending danger of that development, nothing ever can help United States, you may kiss goodbye to your freedom." Bezmenov further states, "Most of the American politicians, media, and educational system trains another generation of people who think they are living at the peacetime. False. United States is in a state of war; undeclared, total war against the basic principles and foundations of this system." A link to the video of Bezmenov's interview can be found at the end of the 'Psychological Warfare' section of '*I THE PEOPLE*'.

IT'S ALL ABOUT ME. ME, ME, ME.

As Ideological Subversion was taking hold, social psychologists were reinventing the individualistic society's cultural construct, self-esteem (self-esteem isn't evidenced in collectivist societies). Behaviorists replaced the introspective nature of self-esteem with that of a subjective nature. In other words, self-esteem was no longer a function of how we saw ourselves, it was now a function of how others saw us and how it affected our feelings. When humanists got ahold of this new definition of self-esteem, now claimed to be a basic human need, and our feelings, they became the central components in personal self-actualization and became pivotal in the diagnosis of psychological disorders.

Even though self-esteem was found to be far less influencial in self-determination than initially thought, beginning in the `70's, government and private sector groups began promoting a self-esteem movement that eventually morphed into a "political correctness" movement to "protect peoples' feelings" by the mid-80's. In 1986 a California assemblyman, John Vasconcellos, created the 'Task Force on Self-Esteem and Personal and Social Responsibility', claiming crime, teen pregnancy, educational under-achievement, and pollution were related to low self-esteem. He alleged that bolstering peoples' self-esteem would insulate them from life's challenges, in turn creating more productive and socially conscious citizens.

In 1995 the task force was scrapped as ineffective. However, the federal government picked up the ball and ran with it, creating the National Council for Self-Esteem and establishing the National Association of Self-Esteem in 2003 that pushed for political correctness in society so peoples' delicate feelings wouldn't be hurt and in turn their now fragile self-esteems wouldn't be crushed.

While Ideological Subversion and the fragile self-esteem was gaining ground in the late `50's/early `60's, a new method of childrearing, championed by the devoutly socialist child psychologist, Dr. Benjamin Spock, was also taking shape. According to him children should be respected, have the same rights as adults, and be allowed a voice in family decisions. He claimed denying them those rights harmed their self-esteem, as did a host of other things he decided hurt their feelings.

Saying "no" to a child was now allegedly as traumatic as a spanking, which was now considered abuse. Children should be "reasoned with" like adults and convinced of the error of their ways, or to do something, with rational conversation; "because I said so" was removed from parents' reportoire of reasons for compliance.

A child's "currency" (toys, attention, etc.) should be found by becoming their friend and used as a tool to attain the parents' desired outcomes, either by negative or positive reinforcement, the harshest negative being a loss of freedom such as a "time out" in their room or loss of their currency. The positive being released from time out, the return of their currency, or the gift of new currency. I've always wondered how one could have a rational conversation with a shrieking two year old. I know you weren't having one with me when I was two, but maybe I was the exception to the rule.

Over the past sixty years Dr. Spock's advice, Ideological Subversion, and the fragile self-esteem has evolved into an "everybody gets a trophy" society where children aren't taught there are winners and losers because losing could hurt their delicate feelings and damage their fragile self-esteems. In essence, preparing the road for the child versus the child for the road, resulting in the creation of terms like "helicopter parenting," to describe over-indulgent parents that believe their children are special and should be society's top priority, hovering over them to protect them from the "evils of the world."

Frequently, when helicopter parented kids experience their first rude awakening when entering adult society they become "boomerang kids" that run home and never leave again. There's also "failure to launch," used to describe selfish, self-absorbed, immature, disrespectful, quasi-adults that refuse to leave their parent's homes and feel they're entitled to mooch off them their entire lives; as well as a recent debate in government over raising the age of adulthood to 24 years of age due to their increasingly evident immaturity. Some parents have actually had to resort to lawsuits and restraining orders in order to force their late thirties/early forties year old children to stop their incessant playing of video games, get jobs, and vacate their basements.

Social media has proven to be a cauldron of selfishness for the self-absorbed entitled young people of today as well as a cavalcade of stupidity in general with every byte of data being stored and used against humanity while being disguised as a "convenience" in order to con people into living their life online in a hyper-escalating cyber-surveillance IoT state. With its follows, likes, and thumbs ups driving stupid people, they entered into a competition to see exactly how stupid they could be almost as soon as social media hit the internet.

Competitors have shown no restraint either, an increasingly alarming number has streamed every stupid or abhorrent activity known to man, including murder, on Facebook Live and when someone's unhappy with anything/anyone now the first thing they do is take to social media to complain, threaten, insult, berate, or belittle (now called cyber-bullying) the subject of their ire, occasionally resulting in the direst of consequences for the most inconsequential reasons due to the learned fragility of peoples' psyches.

The creators of social media claimed it would "connect people" when they first rolled it out, but it's proven to do the exact opposite; alienating, dividing, and isolating people and adding to the dehumanization and devolution of society. People are so obsessed with their smartphones they have no time for each other, nor can they do anything that requires two hands or constant attention because they're always staring at their phones.

Language has also taken a hard hit as people are now talking and writing in "text speech," an abreviated form of language used to make texting quicker. More than 1000 people are injured and at least nine adults and eleven teens die every day in the U.S. due to distracted driving because their phones have become the most important thing in their lives.

Another component of Ideological Subversion is the disintegration of the family unit, the foundation of any society. The family is the beginning of, and the most important part of, the enculturation of every member of a society. It is the family unit that teaches the fundamental core values embodied in a successful member of the community. The destruction of the family unit has resulted in 13.6 million single parent homes raising 21 million children.

This translates to social isolation of the parent due to the burdens of work and childrearing, and over-dependence of the child on the parent as it matures, as well as over-indulgence by the parent when the opportunity arises, which often has a negative impact on both, especially the child, who often suffers from a lack of support and supervision due to the parent's time away from home earning an income and compensative coddling when the parent is present. This situation often prevents parent and child from living to their full potential, and very frequently results in brushes with the legal system, including incarceration, or worse, for the child and sometimes the parent, among a myriad of other issues.

PSEUDOSPECIATION

Pseudospeciation is the act of creating an outgroup, or "other," utilizing cultural identifiers. It's been a tactic to create conflict since before man began walking upright. Ancient rulers named outgroups "barbarians" in order to incite their people into conflict with neighboring peoples, often as a diversionary tactic so their people would be too busy fighting their neighbors to question what the ruler was doing, and they would maintain their loyalty to him, especially if "he won," no matter how treacherous he was. Tribism is the act of banding together with other similar individuals to form a group that is easily identified by its culture.

As this civilization became more complex the tribes it divided itself into became more numerous with five abstract concepts being the main dividing lines; wealth (rich versus poor), theology (one religion, cult, or sect versus another), ideology (one social/political system versus another), skin color (black versus white, etc), and nationality (one nation versus another).

In the world we know now, those five cultural concepts have been subdivided into a multitude of tribes involved in some sort of war (rhetorical or physical) with each other for centuries, with the rhetorical and physical often overlapping into all out war, especially when one tribe's resources were dwindling. There has been war somewhere in the world for the past 4720 years with no end in sight and as we destroy our environment it will only increase as our resources decrease.

DO AS I SAY, NOT AS I DO

It's common fact that we're taught to hate. We're not born hating and may not be taught to hate at home or in our earliest years of school, often quite the opposite. However, as we progress in school and become aware of the world we're taught to view others as rivals by what we see, hear, and experience going on around us and actions speak louder than words. The lies of "discovery" teach us that whites brought "civilization" to an inferior primitive world with their imaginary sky-god, corrupt governments, murderous technology, lust for gold/money, and concept of nations from a very early age.

By the time we're in high school our division into tribes is well underway. We're brainwashed into believing that imposing our beliefs on others is a moral duty an imaginary god bestowed upon us; and to see a potential enemy, at the very least a competitor, in every individual and group dissimilar to ours. And, although our leaders frequently use the words diversity and inclusiveness (blatant indicators of tibism) and insist we work together repeatedly in their rhetoric, their actions, especially in government (tribism couldn't be more blatant than when a socialist congress spends three years doing nothing but attacking a corporatist president) and on the world stage, indicate the exact opposite, reinforcing the tribalistic inclinations we're enculturated with when we enter society.

HILEE EJUWKAATED

BEING TAUGHT JUST ENOUGH TO DO A JOB, GET TO AND FROM THAT JOB, WHILE BEING CONDITIONED TO PROVIDE THE CORRECT EMOTIONAL OUTBURST FOR MULTIPLE STIMULI IS INDOCTRINATION NOT EDUCATION.

I got that spelling from someone on Facebook years ago that didn't like something I posted because I "uzed to manee comas" (commas) according to them. The commas they were referring to were actually apostrophies because, as you may've figured out, I write in the vernacular and use a lot of contractions (although it definitely has its place, I always thought the academic format sounded too stuffy, dispassionate, and impersonal). I even created and used double and triple contractions as part of my vernacular writing in '*METH MONSTER*'. When I attempted to point that out to her, she replied with, "im not stoopid im hilee ejuwkaated n i never herd ov thoz."

Sociology is the study of the development, structure, and functioning of societies, and/or social problems. To do this effectively sociologists often establish a methodology to uniformly create statistics, or use existing ones when available, in order to make comparisons over a period of time. Recently, a longitudinal comparison of a multitude of test scores (IQ, S.A.T., A.C.T., etc.) indictated that every successive generation of Americans since The Second World War has been getting dumber and that dumbing down has accelerated since the `60's. Although languages, standardized and vernacular, are fluid there are established patterns (grammar) that can be used as indicators and the deconstruction of those patterns is a strong indicator of the devolution of a society.

Whether intentionally, due to corruption and greed, or more sinister reasons like the unprecedented success of the KGB's Ideological Subversion, the American education system has continually been defunded and gutted since the early sixties, which accounts for the dumbing down mentioned in the previous paragraph, and no one in history has been more blatant in that destruction than Trump and Betsy Devos.

The creation of an ignorant population that's driven by emotion instead of knowledge and incapable of critical thought, that's extremely easy to manipulate with properly crafted propaganda, makes it easy for ideologically corrupt, morally bankrupt, agenda-driven politicians to dictate to the public what they want them to believe and support, as evidenced by the outcome of every election in the past 244 years. The people have bought into the lies of the winners and gotten screwed every single time. Nonetheless, they continue to play the election game, buying into the lies of every successive stable of idiotic candidates, displaying mass insanity by doing the same thing over and over, expecting a different outcome.

While statistics have marked a noticeable decline in the intelligence of Americans for sociologists, the deconstruction of language patterns has marked the devolution of this society for me. I haven't been in a grade school classroom in fifty-seven years, so I can't comment on the current curriculum, but I can tell you Common Core curriculum promotes circular thought which stymies linear critical thought. It negates any hope of having any common sense, something that's now very uncommon. It also confounds the easy assessment of causality by introducing a myriad of often inconsequential variables. No longer is "walks like a duck, quacks like duck, it's a duck" a viable axiom when talking about cause and effect in this society.

Additionally, I've witnessed teachers that can't spell simple words or structure coherent sentences and read incomprehensible classmates' papers while in college. I heard the admonition of professors to write coherently because they graded on spelling, grammar, and punctuation as well as the subject matter in relation to those incomprehensible papers. I've heard and read the deconstruction of language in television, news reports, graphics, and articles that at times seem to be written or spoken by fourth graders (which has become the new norm), long enough to know something's very wrong with our education system and its graduates.

I also think that a S.T.E.M. (science, technology, engineering, math) curriculum isn't an education, it's just indoctrination into a system that benefits the wealthy elite a million times more than the individual, making one just another cog in a machine bent on "can I" while never considering "should I" for one second. Humanity and the environment has taken a backseat to technology and a paycheck and the insane belief that more technology will repair a caustic humanity and a toxic environment grossly overwhelmed by technology.

During mans' transition from animistic hunter-gatherers to sedentary commercial agriculture and the sky-god religions, the religious and ruling elite created and promulgated the most destructive lie that's ever been told to the ignorant masses…mankind is a special entity that's superior to, and in charge of, everything else in this world, including the planet that supports him. For many thousands of years that one incredibly stupid lie has been the driving force behind the systematic technological destruction of every square inch of the planet and its citizens. We have driven hundreds of thousands of species, including many humans, to extinction as we "civilized" and deforested ("managed") over eighty percent of the earth, poisoned over ninety percent of the water, and polluted all the air.

Now, in our infinite stupidity, we "think" we can compensate for that with technologies we haven't yet created while S.T.E.M. indoctrinated fools frantically search for technological answers in the forms of AI, IoT, synthetic chemicals, and robotics that will allow us to continue destroying our environment and each other unhindered by the impact it has on humanity. Well, the planet has other ideas, as we destroy it, it will destroy us, using everything at its disposal, including us (even against ourselves), and we'll be gone long before we sterilize it.

"MAN HAS LOST THE CAPACITY TO FORESEE AND FORESTALL, HE WILL END BY DESTROYING THE EARTH." – Dr. Albert Schweitzer

STUPID PEOPLE ELECT STUPIDER POLITICIANS
"IN AN AGE WHEN MAN HAS FORGOTTEN HIS ORIGINS AND IS BLIND EVEN TO HIS MOST ESSENTIAL NEEDS FOR SURVIVAL, WATER ALONG WITH OTHER RESOURCES HAS BECOME THE VICTIM OF HIS INDIFFERENCE." – Rachel Carson, '*Silent Spring*'

Nothing proves that simple truth better than the soap opera of idiotic, tribalistic, childish, ideologically corrupt, morally bankrupt, squabbling three year olds that claim to be "leaders" and the current climate of agenda driven hatred, petty self-absorbed greedy selfishness, and destructive stupidity that permeate every government on the planet. No one leads those idiocracies better than the current idiot-in-chief, "The Donald," Donald J. Trump. As self-absorbed, hyper-inflated-egomaniacal narcissitic lying idiots go, he's in a class of his own, with Xi Jinping first as communist dictators go, being a close second after Trump in blatant stupidity and Jair Bolsonaro in third place but working diligently to attain first.

At least most world leaders pretend to be concerned with the destruction of the planet. Not these three, Trump "thinks" climate change is a hoax created by China/Xi to ruin American manufacturing, while Xi and Bolsonaro have dedicated themselves to turning the South American continent into a desert. Bolsonaro won his Brazilian Presidency by promising the agricultural/ranching and mining industries free reign to indiscriminantly level the Amazon Rainforest, the singularly most important ecosystem for man's survival on the planet, for the sake of the money a few cows and some rare earth elements will bring.

More recently, Bolsonaro has proven he's attained a level of stupidity rarely seen, even in Trump, by making disparaging remarks about Brigette Macron when the president of France, Emmanuel Macron, offered to send help to fight the Brazilian wildfires Bolsonaro denies the existence of, while blaming Leonardo Di Caprio for paying activists to set the allegedly non-existant fires.

Xi's "Made in China 2025" and "Belt and Road Iniative" aren't only about cornering the global manufacturing market, that's actually secondary to creating a global totalitarian state run by "The Party" where

China/Xi controls every aspect of everyones' life via the algorithmically governed social crediting system already in place in China.

Unfortunately, fifty-eight countries are already onboard. You'd be amazed at the percentage of what you believe to be "the free world" China already owns and what it's in the process of acquiring through traitorous proxies and deceptive monetary assistance that ultimately leads to political leverage. Not only is China dedicated to paving every square inch of the planet and stripping South America of its resources, it's been working diligently to do the same in Africa for decades. It's even built, as yet unpopulated, "ghost cities" that can house millions in preparation of their impending total takeover.

CONNECTING THE DOTS

By now I'm sure you're wondering, if you're still reading this, what the previous eleven sections can possibly have to do with the escalating violence in the world, especially mass shootings. After all, according to your favorite puppet(s), it's all the guns' fault. Thinking that if there weren't any guns there wouldn't be any killing is as ridiculous as thinking if there weren't any spoons obesity wouldn't exist. Blaming inanimate objects for society's problems is your idiotic politicians' stock in trade unless they can find someone from another tribe to blame.

People bent on killing will always find a way to carry out their plans, it's as simple as that, and the more we destroy our environment the more people bent on killing there will be. By blaming inanimate objects politicians think they can duck out of taking responsibility for the adverse effects their idiotic policies have had and they can shirk accountability for their stupidity.

Now, let's get to the intersections of the previous eleven sections that are the cause(s) of the escalating violence in the world. But, before we do I've gotta tell you, again…as the planet is destroyed we will be too, by our own hand, as well as every other creature that's capable and the planet itself. Historically, escalating violence has been a reaction to the perception of dwindling resources, and every resource mankind has exploited is disappearing rapidly.

Every tribe on the planet wants to be first and longest at the rapidly emptying trough, as that trough empties the violence will grow and no laws or restrictions will even slow it down. Laws are just ink on paper and only have the power we allow them. When pressed by extinction, laws become meaningless. This planet is as much a living entity as the creatures that populate it. It will exterminate us before it will allow us to sterilize it.

Via the "better living through chemistry" policy every successive generation for the past sixty years has been exposed to escalating levels of neurotoxins that are stored in fatty tissues, which is primarily what our brains are composed of, and carcinogens that form cancer causing free radicals that attack the weakest genes, resulting in genetic mutations that compound with every successive generation creating a myriad of detrimental physiological defects affecting the physicality and mentality of each individual in each generation, as well as a growing list of cancers…

"THE CONTAMINATION OF OUR WORLD IS NOT ALONE A MATTER OF MASS SPRAYING. INDEED, FOR MOST OF US THIS IS OF LESS IMPORTANCE THAN THE INNUMERABLE SMALL-SCALE EXPOSURES TO WHICH WE ARE SUBJECTED DAY BY DAY, YEAR AFTER YEAR. LIKE THE CONSTANT DRIPPING OF WATER THAT WEARS AWAY THE HARDEST STONE, THIS BIRTH-TO-DEATH CONTACT WITH DANGEROUS CHEMICALS MAY IN THE END PROVE DISASTROUS. EACH OF THESE RECURRENT EXPOSURES, NO MATTER HOW SLIGHT, CONTRIBUTES TO THE PROGRESSIVE BUILDUP OF CHEMICALS IN OUR BODIES AND SO TO CUMULATIVE POISONING."
– Rachel Carson, *Silent Spring*

These mutations are responsible for a plethora of genetic, birth, physical, and neurological defects such as Compromised/Diminished Immune Systems, Autoimmune Diseases, Cleft Palate, Spina Bifida, Trisomy Syndromes, Gastroschisis, Anencephaly, Congenital Heart Defects, Hypoplastic Left Heart Syndrome, Encephalocele, Omphalocele, Clubfoot, Microencephaly, and Neural Tube Defect, with relatively new and currently "rare" genetic diseases like A.F.M. (Acute Flaccid Myelitis) becoming increasingly prevalent, to name but a few of the five thousand plus known genetic diseases…

"THE ORGANIC PHOSPHATES, USUALLY CONSIDERED ONLY IN RELATION TO THEIR MORE VIOLENT MANIFESTATIONS IN ACUTE POISONING, ALSO HAVE THE POWER TO PRODUCE LASTING PHYSICAL DAMAGE TO NERVE TISSUES AND, ACCORDING TO RECENT FINDINGS, TO INDUCE MENTAL HEALTH DISORDERS." –
Rachel Carson, *Silent Spring*

STUDY: SOY-FED INFANTS HAVE DIFFERENCES IN REPRODUCTIVE SYSTEM TISSUES
The full story: https://www.news-medical.net/news/20180313/Study-Soy-fed-infants-have-differences-in-reproductive-system-tissues.aspx

March 13, 2018

Infants who consumed soy-based formula as newborns had differences in some reproductive-system cells and tissues, compared to those who used cow-milk formula or were breastfed, according to a new study. The researchers say the differences, measured in the months after birth, were subtle and not a cause for alarm, but reflect a need to further investigate the long-term effects of exposure to estrogen-like compounds found in soy-based formulas. "Soy formula contains high concentrations of plant-based estrogen-like compounds, and because this formula is the sole food source for many babies in the first six months of life, it's important to understand the effects of exposure to such compounds during a critical period in development," said Virginia A. Stallings, MD, director of the Nutrition Center at Children's Hospital of Philadelphia (CHOP). Stallings is a senior author of a new study published online March 1 in the Journal of Clinical Endocrinology and Metabolism.

The mutations are also responsible for multiple mental health disorders such as Substance Abuse, Impulse Control Disorders, Personality Disorders, Gender Dysphoria (especially in children fed soy-based formulas), ADHD, Autism, Mood Disorders, Eating Disorders, Anxiety Disorders, Alzheimers, Dementia, and Parkinsons. Geneticists have also found direct correlations between specific cancers and the environmental carcinogens the subjects were exposed to…

"LULLED BY THE SOFT SELL AND THE HIDDEN PERSUADER, THE AVERAGE CITIZEN IS SELDOM AWARE OF THE DEADLY MATERIALS WITH WHICH HE IS SURROUNDING HIMSELF; INDEED, HE MAY NOT REALIZE HE IS USING THEM AT ALL." – Rachel Carson, '*Silent Spring*'

I'LL SHOW YOU!

Coddled, over-indulged children of over-protective parents that have been taught the pain of hurt feelings is equal to or greater than physical pain without ever really experiencing either; whose worst "consequence" has been losing their Xbox for a week, grow up to be self-absorbed, selfish, immature quasi-adults that can't handle rejection, criticism, or being told 'no'. They lash out violently when it happens because they have poor to no impulse control, diminished to no rational thought capabilties, and a myriad of personality and mood disorders due to conditioning and mutations of their brains, especially the frontal lobes, that often allow a propensity for violence to become the norm.

As they proceed through the enculturation/indoctrination system they form ingroups/tribes (cliques) of similar circumstanced individuals, often harassing to the point of violence outgroups and those dissimilar to themselves, which is strongly reinforced by the childish tribism displayed by our goverment and every portion of adult society. With the least stable pyschologically, often committing simple suicide, or the latest trend, suicide by mass shooting, a modernized version of suicide by cop that gains them more notority, especially on their best friend, social media.

There's been a lot of debate about the affect violent video games have on chronic players. Some say they desensitize players, others disagree. I don't think it's that players are desensitized. I think it's because they've rarely been seriously injured in their lives; their delicate feelings have been hurt but they have no idea what real pain is, and are curious how it would "feel" to actually inflict pain and kill people. They're especially curious since violence is glorified in all forms of media, entertainment, and real life where war is glorified, soldiers are considered heros, and hero cops kill bad guys, and the occasional good guy, every day in real life and on TV.

I also think they believe "going down in a blaze of glory," taking as many others with them as possible, will show all their detractors they're better than simply committing suicide because they couldn't handle life. They choose those they consider "normal" to victimize because they feel incapable of successfully coping with what life throws at them, as they believe their victims can. They lash out at the unaware and defenseless assuming they'll finally have the upper hand when making their statement, which is that they want others to hurt as much as they feel they do.

That they choose a certain group to attack is secondary unless their attack is retribution against their detractors, such as student on student shootings, which are a more direct result of the suppression of a baser instinct when it first arises at a very young age. Allowing a first grade playground spat to continue to resolution can head off a more serious event down the road for several reasons, as discussed in ITP.

One thing all mass shooters have in common is that at some point in their enculturation they were deemed "weird" by their peers and ostracized and/or relegated to the clique of "weird" kids where they were often further marginalized for one reason or another, often becoming loners that harbor a multitude of grudges against the "normal" kids and "normal" society in general. As they matured their grudge morphed into outright hatred that became murderous as soon as they chose a group to vent their anger on. The rhetoric or propaganda the "experts" point to as the cause is just the excuse they chose in an attempt to rationalize their abhorent behavior and transform it into "heroism" in their mind.

VIOLENCE IS THE SANCTUARY OF THE IDIOCRACY.

The perfect storm of Ideological Subversion, genetic mutations, constant exposure to a plethora of neurotoxins, tribism, leaders' divisive rhetoric and lies, a myriad of ists and isms (racist, racism, facsist, facism, etc.), excessive permissiveness, a lack of consequences, coddling, under-education, self-absorption, the equating of violence to heroism, attention seeking, idolization of stupidity, and a sense of diminishing resources have created an idiocratic society prone to irrational thoughts, actions, and violence.

A DISPOSABLE WORLD

Enter, a brave new world governed by the stupidest people available that squabble like three year olds over inconsequential drivel and their versions of ideological corruption; where coddled self-absorbed kids have become selfish immature quasi-adults that are hurt by words and deal with rejection or disagreement by lashing out violently against those that rejected or disagreed with them, shooting up public places, and/or committing suicide; where feelings and beliefs have replaced facts and knowledge; blatant lies are unashamedly passed off as truth, especially by those in leadership positions; everyone demands protection from themselves while refusing to take responsibility for their actions; ignorance and stupidity have become admired, emulated, and sought after, while intelligence and common sense have become contemptable; where wrong is right (especially if it goes viral and attracts followers, likes, and money), right is non-existent, and empty promises, or hollow rhetoric, carry more weight than actions, or lack thereof; where people cry about mass shootings when 1000 people a day are injured and killed because people can't put their stupid phones down long enough to drive across town safely; where thirty-one percent of people don't know their neighbors because their best friend is a device…

"THIS IS AN ERA OF SPECIALISTS, EACH OF WHOM SEES HIS OWN PROBLEM AND IS UNAWARE OF OR INTOLERANT OF THE LARGER FRAME INTO WHICH IT FITS. IT IS ALSO AN ERA DOMINATED BY INDUSTRY, IN WHICH THE RIGHT TO MAKE A DOLLAR AT WHATEVER THE COST IS SELDOM CHALLENGED. WHEN THE PUBLIC PROTESTS, CONFRONTED WITH SOME OBVIOUS EVIDENCE OF DAMAGING RESULTS OF PESTICIDE APPLICATIONS, IT IS FED

LITTLE TRANQUILIZING PILLS OF HALF–TRUTH." – Rachel Carson, *'Silent Spring'*
This also applies to the lies told about natural gas and fracking.

"THE OBLIGATION TO ENDURE GIVES US THE RIGHT TO KNOW." – Jean Rostand

A world that's being exterminated/polluted/poisoned by converting everything in it to worthless pieces of paper that the few ultra-wealthy consider themselves geniuses for creating and hoarding and have elevated themselves to the status of gods in their own minds and those of their peers because of it…

"BUT MAN IS A PART OF NATURE, AND HIS WAR AGAINST NATURE IS INEVITABLY A WAR AGAINST HIMSELF." – Rachel Carson

The ridiculous belief that we were created by an omnipresent imaginary sky-god to act as his surrogate caretakers of this planet has resulted in an incredibly arrogant assumption that we're the masters of this world. When in actuality, we're an integral part of a biological entity, much like cells are integral parts of our body, that has taken on the the characteristics of a virus, or a cancer, and overwhelmed our host…

WHEN OUR ACTIVITIES ARE VIEWED ACROSS TIME IT'S VERY EASY TO COME TO THE CONCLUSION WE'RE NOTHING MORE THAN THE MOST ADVANCED VIRUS ON THE PLANET.

"NATURE HAS INTRODUCED A GREAT VARIETY INTO THE LANDSCAPE, BUT MAN HAS DISPLAYED A PASSION FOR SIMPLIFYING IT. THUS HE UNDOES THE BUILT-IN CHECKS AND BALANCES BY WHICH NATURE HOLDS THE SPECIES WITHIN BOUNDS." Rachel Carson, *'Silent Spring'*

THE PROPAGANDA OF THE ELITE DEMANDS WE RESPECT THE DIVERSITY OF OUR SPECIES WHILE WE DESTROY THE DIVERSITY OF EVERY OTHER SPECIES AND OUR ENVIRONMENT.

For that we will pay the ultimate price, extinction, if we don't stop listening to the greedy idiots we've allowed to lead us into an unwinnable war with our environment and in turn each other. As we attempt to replace biology with technology we will only succeed in exterminating ourselves. We're well on the way to that end now and as we get closer we'll only get more violent despite all the lip-service of the experts and the ineffective laws politicians make. Life always finds a way, even if it has to exterminate everything and start over. Mankind's legacy will be nothing more than extinction and a gigantic pile of trash if we continue listening to the greedy power-mad idiots that brought us to this juncture.

"THE HUMAN RACE IS CHALLENGED MORE THAN EVER BEFORE TO DEMONSTRATE OUR MASTERY, NOT OVER NATURE BUT OF OURSELVES." – Rachel Carson

"MAN CAN HARDLY EVEN RECOGNIZE THE DEVILS OF HIS OWN CREATION." – Dr. Albert Schweitzer

"AS CRUDE A WEAPON AS THE CAVEMAN'S CLUB, A CHEMICAL BARRAGE HAS BEEN HURLED AGAINST THE FABRIC OF LIFE – A FABRIC ON ONE HAND DELICATE AND DESTRUCTIBLE, ON THE OTHER MIRACULOUSLY TOUGH AND RESILIENT, AND CAPABLE OF STRIKING BACK IN UNEXPECTED WAYS." – Rachel Carson, '*Silent Spring*'

ESCAPE FROM THE LAND OF DELUSION
"IN ORDER TO GAIN ANYTHING, YOU MUST FIRST LOSE EVERYTHING." – Siddhartha Gautama, Buddha

"WHOEVER HAS AT SOME TIME BUILT A "NEW HEAVEN" HAS FOUND THE POWER TO DO SO ONLY IN HIS *OWN HELL*." – Friedrich Nietzsche, *On the Genealogy of Morals*

"WHEN MENDACIOUSNESS AT ANY PRICE MONOPOLIZES THE WORD "TRUTH" FOR ITS PERSPECTIVE, THE REALLY TRUTHFUL MAN IS BOUND TO BE BRANDED WITH THE WORST NAMES" – Freidrich Nietzsche, *Ecce Homo*

"WHEN TRUTH ENTERS INTO A FIGHT WITH THE LIES OF MILLENNIA, WE SHALL HAVE UPHEAVALS, A CONVULSION OF EARTHQUAKES, A MOVING OF MOUNTAINS AND VALLEYS, THE LIKE OF WHICH HAS NEVER BEEN DREAMED OF. THE CONCEPT OF POLITICS WILL HAVE MERGED ENTIRELY WITH A WAR OF SPIRITS; ALL POWER STRUCTURES OF THE OLD SOCIETY WILL HAVE BEEN EXPLODED – ALL OF THEM ARE BASED ON LIES: THERE WILL BE WARS THE LIKE OF WHICH HAVE NEVER YET BEEN SEEN ON EARTH." – Freidrich Nietzsche, *Ecce Homo, Why I Am A Destiny, sec.1*

WE CAN DO THIS. IN FACT, WE CAN DO ANYTHING IF WE DO IT TOGETHER.

OVERCOMING HUMANITY'S OVERWHELMINGLY DEEP ENTRENCHMENT IN TRIBISM WILL BE THE MOST DIFFICULT PART OF EXECUTING ANY PLAN FOR REAL CHANGE. NONETHELESS, NOTHING WILL CHANGE IF EVERYTHING ISN'T CHANGED.

THE KEY

If we're gonna change this world a comprehensive education is the singularly most important component of that change. Everyone needs a fact-based education in the truth of who we are, where we come from, and where we're headed if we don't change. That means ending all the ridiculous myths and lies about god(s), messiahs, prophets, creation, divinity, and everything that's built on those lies like monarchies, religions, idiotic beliefs, and governments/corporations that continuously prattle on about being net zero carbon by 2040, for example.

Along with the truth of everything, everyone will need to learn what it will take to become a totally autonomous entity capable of sustaining one's self and domicile without any aid, which entails learning all the new systems that will be employed, as well as gardening, nutrition, and biomedicine to name but a few.

How it will be accomplished will be revealed in brief generalities as we proceed through the components required to implement each change in the following narrative. The various components of the new paradigm discussed here are just the beginning end results (once everyone's on the same footing there shouldn't be any end results, progress should be continual). Exactly how we're gonna get there will be determined by a myriad of variables that will have to be addressed as we get to them in each area they're being executed. The most difficult of which will be the first. With that in mind, I would suggest we begin in rural areas. That way we'll have quite a bit of experience and be on the same page when we get to the most difficult areas, the cities.

IN THE BEGINNING

I provided this article in full because this is a major issue that has to be addressed and resolved before we can move forward with a pivotal component of the plan to restore balance to the world and it has to be done as quickly as possible, we're running out of time. And, no I don't advocate for nuclear energy, just the opposite.

CLEAN ENERY'S DIRTY LITTLE SECRET
Discarded solar panels are piling up all over the world, and they represent a major threat to the environment. Clean energy may not be so clean after all.

By Julie Kelly.
Find it here: https://www.nationalreview.com/2017/06/solar-panel-waste-environmental-threat-clean-energy/
June 28th 2017

A new study by Environmental Progress (EP) warns that toxic waste from used solar panels now poses a global environmental threat. The Berkeley-based group found that solar panels create 300 times more toxic waste per unit of energy than nuclear power plants. Discarded solar panels, which contain dangerous elements such as lead, chromium, and cadmium, are piling up around the world, and there's been little done to mitigate their potential danger to the environment.

"We talk a lot about the dangers of nuclear waste, but that waste is carefully monitored, regulated, and disposed of," says Michael Shellenberger, founder of Environmental Progress, a nonprofit that advocates for the use of nuclear energy. "But we had no idea there would be so many panels — an enormous amount — that could cause this much ecological damage."

Solar panels are considered a form of toxic, hazardous electronic or "e-waste," and according to EP researchers Jemin Desai and Mark Nelson, scavengers in developing countries like India and China often "burn the e-waste in order to salvage the valuable copper wires for resale. Since this process requires burning off plastic, the resulting smoke contains toxic fumes that are carcinogenic and teratogenic (birth defect-causing) when inhaled." This is one of the dirty little secrets behind the push for renewable energy.

While consumers might view solar panels as harmless little windows made from glass and plastic, the reality is that they are intricately constructed from a variety of materials, making it difficult to disassemble and recycle them. Japan is already scrambling for ways to reuse its mounting inventory of solar-panel waste, which is expected to exceed 10,000 tons by 2020 and grow by 700,000 to 800,000 tons per year by 2040. Solutions are hard to find, due both to the labor-intensive process of breaking down the panels and to the low price of scrap.

(Dan Whitten, a spokesman for the Solar Energy Industries Association, disputes EP's study. In an e-mail to me, he claims that solar panels are "mainly made up of easy-to-recycle materials that can be successfully recovered and reused at the end of their useful life.") This

will also be a problem here in the U.S., which has more than 1.4 million solar-energy installations now in use, including many already near the end of their 25-year lifespan.

Federal and state governments have been slow to enact disposal and recycling policies, undoubtedly fearful of raising any red flags about the environmental threat posed by a purported climate-change panacea. Meanwhile, at precisely the moment when, because of the rise of smartphones, Americans are generating less waste from consumer electronics, discarded solar panels are stacking up. EP estimates that Americans with solar roofs produce 30 to 60 percent more electronic waste than non-solar households.

Thankfully, renewable-energy sources are at last facing some much-needed scrutiny, even within the ranks of green activists. "At a time when iPhones have reduced our need for digital cameras, alarm clocks, GPS systems, and other electronics, solar panels risk increasing overall e-waste production," Shellenberger says. "The people who could pay the price for this hazard are some of the poorest people in the world."

This is not to even mention the environmental damage done by making solar panels in the first place. A 2013 investigation by the Associated Press found that from 2007 to 2011, the manufacture of solar panels in California "produced 46.5 million pounds of sludge and contaminated water. Roughly 97 percent of it was taken to hazardous waste facilities throughout the state, but more than 1.4 million pounds were transported to nine other states." That's no way for a state to keep its carbon footprint small; one renewable-energy analyst quoted by the AP estimated it would take "one to three months of generating electricity [from the solar panels] to pay off the energy invested in driving those hazardous waste emissions out of state."

Six years later, it's safe to assume the amount of toxic waste is even higher as solar-panel production continues to ramp up. Thankfully, renewable-energy sources are at last facing some much-needed scrutiny, even within the ranks of green activists. A group of prominent scientists recently rebuked a study by Mark Jacobson, a Stanford professor and leading clean-energy (and anti-nuclear) activist, who had claimed that the U.S. could generate energy exclusively from wind, water, and solar energy by the year 2050.

The scientists said Jacobson's study "used invalid modeling tools, contained modeling errors, and made implausible and inadequately supported assumptions." The group admonished policymakers to "treat with caution any visions of a rapid, reliable, and low-cost transition to entire energy systems that relies almost exclusively on wind, solar, and hydroelectric power."

As the Trump administration considers reforming federal energy subsidies, officials should look at how renewable technologies such as solar panels impact the environment once they've outlived their usefulness. ***There is nothing environmentally friendly about creating mountains of hazardous waste in an effort to reduce CO2 emissions****.*

What we'll have to do is find a way to create solar panels with an infinite lifespan that require no toxic materials for their manufacture. An answer to that may already be available in the transparent panels mentioned in another article excerpt further on in this work.

The following emboldened paragraph is the summation of CNN's article on the latest climate change revelation that gives the world a twelve-year window to make many drastic changes in our activities on this planet or suffer a catastrophic climate event (catastrophic climate events are already happening around the globe, just ask the people from Paradise, CA. or any one of hundreds of places that have been inundated by ultra-destructive hurricanes, tornadoes, earthquakes, tsunamis, volcanic eruptions, heatwaves/wildfires, and polar vortexes that are getting successively worse).

Our only solution – "collective human action is required to steer us away from this potential threshold, including "decarbonization" of the global economy, enhancement of biosphere carbon sinks, behavioral changes, technological innovations, new governance arrangements, and transformed social values." – CNN

I don't agree with the twelve-year timeline because the climatologists that made that assessment haven't taken what I call the 'snowball effect' into account. Until now that is; they recently discovered that the Arctic ice pack is melting forty to sixty percent faster than they predicted and Antarctica is melting sixteen times faster. I maintain we have five years till a cataclysmic event severely impacts, if not negates, the chances of continued human existence due to the snowball effect, which is simply that as the environment deteriorates the deterioration accelerates, as exemplified by the accelerating devolution of mankind.

The Covid-19 release is an indication of that devolution. One incredibly authoritarian group of global elites, with Xi Jinping as their front man, "think" he and his Chinese communists should rule the entire world. To that end they released a biological agent on the world that won't be stopped easily, if at all, which is designed to spread quickly, mutate around any vaccine or immunity, and proliferate in any environment in order to wipe out a major amount of the population to curtail any potent resistance to their agenda. And, they're counting on the sheer self-absorbed stupidity of Trump to inadvertently assist them in nullifying those whom they consider their greatest adversary.

The rest of this book is the plan that addresses all the things in the previous emboldened paragraph as well as every aspect of the devolution of humankind.

YOU SHOULD UNDERSTAND FIRST AND FOREMOST THAT THERE IS NO BOILERPLATE FIX FOR THE DESTRUCTION THE GREED OF THE ELITE HAS WROUGHT ON THE PLANET AND ITS CITIZENS. THE FOLLOWING IS NOT TO BE CONSIDERED AS SUCH BECAUSE EVERY IDEA WILL HAVE TO BE ADAPTED TO THE REGION AND CULTURE IN WHICH IT'S EMPLOYED.

The following details a critical plan that I doubt anyone will be willing to undertake until all else has failed because the "experts" will insist that if they're allowed to piecemeal tinker with the current paradigm long enough they'll hit on something that works eventually, while they actually continue on with their plan that's been in progress for several thousand years, and sadly, people will believe it. They don't know any better and it's much easier to sit back and let someone else lie to them than question it and be vilified as a dissenter by the moronic majority on social media.

Additionally, this plan will require a major change in the intelligence level of the individual globally so society can begin to work together on a collective level. However, due to the deep indoctrination in money, religion, government, and race and the amount of work it will require from everyone I doubt more than a handful of people will even consider it. The moronic majority, including the current power structure, will label it excessive, impossible, and me a nut case. However, as I said in the opening of *'I THE PEOPLE'* it will at least be available as a starting point when the need for a drastic alternative is finally recognized, if humankind survives long enough that it ever is.

APPLY THE KISS THEORY
K.I.S.S. theory = **K**eep **I**t **S**imple **S**tupid

Keeping everything as simple as absolutely possible so that's it's easy to build, adapt, maintain, and replicate wherever and whenever needed will go a long way towards making everyone and their home self-sufficient in that no one will have to wait for an "expert" to repair or replace a failed system. They'll be able to have that system up and running within hours after its failure on their own. One will be able to access tutorials and parts suppliers through their televisions, computers, or devices to that end. More later.

When confronted or questioned about policies, whether good or bad, politicians frequently dodge a direct answer by claiming "it's complicated" or we wouldn't understand if they explained it to us, or by talking around in circles for fifteen minutes while saying absolutely nothing. Life is only as complicated as it's made by the powers that be. Making it complicated ensures that laymen will never understand an issue, and in this dumbed-down society people don't even bother to think or question anything anymore because it's easier to just go where their favorite "leaders" take them than ask why we're headed in the wrong direction. Simplifying everything will ensure everyone's on the same footing and capable of making good decisions in all aspects of their lives, as well as their communal and global lives too.

If you paid attention to 'The Protocols' in ITP it shouldn't be difficult to notice that everything in this plan is in direct opposition to the things underlined there. Additionally, besides the direct opposition, the K.I.S.S. theory has been applied to each solution to make it easy for everyone to participate in. I strongly doubt it will happen now because it will require the acceptance of responsibility, a lot of work from everyone, and a total paradigm shift in how we think and behave, especially towards the planet and each other.

A COMMON MISCONCEPTION

The most common statement made when I mention changing the paradigm, besides "I don't know what a paradigm is," is that people immediately assume everything's just gonna vanish and we'll be starting over from scratch. When the guard changes at Buckingham Palace it doesn't disappear and have to be rebuilt all over again each time. The reality is, not much in our material world will change. Your vehicle will still be in the driveway, your La-Z-Boy will still be in front of your TV, and all your possessions will actually be yours instead of the bank's or the government's. The only thing that will happen initially is that everything will be free, or more precisely, the currency will change from money to participation, that'll be the first thing you'll notice.

Then, if you have loved ones off fighting somewhere, you'll probably notice they're home. You might notice there are no homeless people on the streets. Maybe you'll even feel the anxiety that's built up over the years begin to fade away. You may even want to watch the news because it's good for a change and you want to be a part of it. I guarantee that every change we make will have an instant effect and a ripple effect throughout civilization as we move toward homeostasis and that will multiply with every step we take.

I can't stress enough that we're the ones that make the world turn, not the people that turn us on each other. Without their money they're absolutely nothing, without them, we're still everything. We can simply walk away from them, their monopoly money, fake religions, corrupt governments, and divisive propaganda and there's nothing they can do but watch us go. There doesn't need to be any energy wasted in fighting, protesting, rallies, marches, demonstrations, or anything they've created in order to make you believe you're "doing something" while having a contingency for controlling every avenue of your dissent. We simply exclude them from our society unless they're willing to change too.

THE ONLY WAY TO REVERSE THE EFFECT OF AN ACTIVITY IS REVERSE, OR STOP, THE ACTIVITY.

The following will be in as much a conversational format as possible, like ITP, maybe a little more so since this is the solution portion of the message and this portion is strictly my own based on 64 years of being human and finding out why. Although this is laid out in what seems to be a sequential format that appears the shift will be performed in steps, the reality is the shift will happen concurrently and many of the things will have to happen as simultaneously as possible.

Additionally, it's not gonna happen overnight. We're gonna be starting with baby-steps as we drop thousands of years of conditioning and begin working together, but as we progress the speed with which we accomplish things will increase. Nothing will be easy and there's gonna be a lot of on-the-job training but we're humans, we can do anything we put our minds and shoulders to.

That being said, my strategy here is that we begin a project together on the familial level and once we're all up to speed on it on the communal level we dedicate a portion of us to continue that project while others move on to assist in other similar projects in other communities and we do this until all of us are working on as many projects as possible. As a group finishes their project, they reassign themselves to other projects in the works till we finish that group of projects then we move on to the next group of projects in a similar fashion until everyone's on the exact same footing and has everything they need to thrive.

PROGRESS ONLY HAPPENS OUTSIDE ONE'S COMFORT ZONE.

MATRICENTRISM = Earthcentric Collective Individualism (mindfulness)

Earthcentric = A society organized around the **mother**, that mother being **Earth**, our environment, the planet we live on, you know, the one we can't live without; the one we're trashing every day at an alarmingly increasing rate, the one we've already trashed eighty percent of the surface of, and ninety percent of the water, yah, that one. The one most people won't give a flying fuck about till it's gone.

Collective = A loosely knit, closely connected social organization based on a premise of being as equally responsible for the one to the left and right of you as you are to yourself. That ensures that no less than three people are working in one's favor at any given time.

Individualism = One is responsible for one's self, first and foremost, but not exclusively, and only till all one's needs are satisfied, with one's community being next in line.

THE CURRENT FORM OF SOCIAL ORGANIZATION EXISTS ONLY BECAUSE WE PARTICIPATE IN IT. IT WOULD DIE IN ONE HOUR WITHOUT US. WE ARE THE POWER, NOT THE FEW ELITES THAT MANIPULATE US; WITHOUT US THEY COULDN'T SURVIVE, NEITHER COULD THEIR SYSTEM.

PATRIARCHY IS INHERENTLY UNEQUAL. FURTHER INEQUALITY IS THE ONLY THING A SYSTEM BASED ON INEQUALITY CAN BREED. THERE'S NOTHING ABOUT PATRIARCHY THAT CAN BE "FIXED," IT'S WORKING PERFECTLY. RESTRUCTURING THE SYSTEM IS THE ONLY SOLUTION.

"A JOURNEY OF A THOUSAND MILES BEGINS WITH A SINGLE STEP." – Lao Tzu
Each step shortens the journey.

<u>"You never change things by fighting the existing reality. To change something, build a new model that makes the old model obsolete"</u> –
R. Buckminster Fuller

Fallibilism is the philosophical doctrine that all claims of knowledge could, in principal, be mistaken, but I may be wrong. The "open society" basically refers to a "test and evaluate" (piecemeal tinkering) approach to social engineering. Regarding "open society" Roy Childs writes, "Since the Second World War, most of the Western democracies have followed Karl Popper's advice about piecemeal social engineering and democratic social reform, and it has gotten them into a grand mess." Popperism will be ended and a comprehensive failure-proof approach that includes every citizen of the planet will be instituted.

THE PROBLEM
WASTE MORE, WANT MORE
The imbalance between our natural environment and our technological environment is increasingly more toxic as technology overwhelms biology in the insane pursuit of more. That toxicity is now manifesting in the creatures on the planet, especially humans. Many species are dying in massive numbers, people are going insane, killing each other in droves, and the planet has initiated its extermination protocol, as evidenced by the increasingly severe weather and natural disasters like volcanic eruptions, earth quakes, tornadoes, and hurricanes as we suck the life out of our environment in the insane quest for more and better technological trinkets.

THE CAUSE
"HOLDING BACK THE RICHES OF EARTH, SEA, AND SKY FROM THE FELLOWS WHO FAMISH AND FREEZE IN THE DARK, THEY [THE SYNDICATES AND TRUSTS]…ASSERT THE RIGHT, FOR THEIR PRIVATE PROFIT, TO REGULATE THE CONSUMPTION BY THE PEOPLE OF THE NECESSARIES OF LIFE, AND TO CONTROL PRODUCTION, NOT BY THE NEEDS OF HUMANITY, BUT THE DESIRES OF FEW FOR DIVIDENDS." – Henry Demarest Lloyd, *Wealth against Commonwealth*

A few hundred ultra-greedy people claim to own or control everything on the planet and consider everything and everyone but themselves and theirs collateral damage as they exploit everything and everyone in their maniacal quest to convert everything on, and in, the planet to useless strips of paper they consider themselves brilliant for creating, hoarding, and manipulating the rest of the world and its inhabitants with. All the while, this conversion is destroying the very biosphere we require to exist and as it degrades so does everything the biosphere nourishes, hence the societal devolution that's become major news.

A gross simplification of the elite's monetary system: they create the money out of nothing, assign it a base value and an interest rate before it's even dry; loan it at interest to governments to circulate; through payments, fees, taxes, purchases, and a myriad of trickery like insurance and usury, the money eventually ends up being hoarded in the bank accounts of the same people that created it and the governments go ever further into debt, indebting us too, making us debt-slaves to a system most people don't even understand.

THE SOLUTION
NULLIFICATION

In order to nullify the elite's power, we must end the following tools of control they use to keep us subservient, divided, and squabbling about the non-issues they fabricate to keep society at each other's throats.

END THE WORSHIP OF MONEY
WHEN A SOCIETY'S STRUCTURE IS BASED ON MONEY SO IS ITS DISPARITIES.

In case you've missed something, everything in this world revolves around money. It's become the most powerful control mechanism the elite possess, hence its continual mention. Even the fake religions that once claimed to worship the imaginary sky-god now openly worship money above all else with their snake oil salesmen (preachers) being some of the richest people in the world. And, let's never forget the elite's governments of squabbling, ideologically corrupt, morally bankrupt idiots that only have one thing on their minds, how to appropriate as much money as they can without the people knowing while maintaining their fake appearance of intelligence, honesty, and decorum.

WORLD INEQUALITY GROWS AMID GLUT OF NEW BILLIONAIRES, OXFAM SAYS

By Shelly Hagan. For the full article: https://www.bloomberg.com/news/articles/2018-01-22/world-inequality-grows-amid-glut-of-new-billionaires-oxfam-says
Jan 21st 2018

The global economy created a record number of billionaires last year, exacerbating inequality amid a weakening of workers' rights and a corporate push to maximize shareholder returns, charity organization Oxfam International said in a new report. The world now has 2,043 billionaires, after a new one emerged every two days in the past year, the nonprofit organization said in a report published Monday. The group of mostly men saw its wealth surge by $762 billion, which is enough money to end extreme poverty seven times over, according to Oxfam.

THE INSANE LUST FOR MONEY WILL END WITH OUR EXTERMINATION.

<u>Money exists to be circulated and any kind of stagnation of money acts ruinously on the running of the state machinery, for which it is</u>

the lubricant; a stagnation of the lubricant may stop the regular working of the mechanism - Protocol 20, line 15

Economic crises have been produced by us for the goyim by no other means than the withdrawal of money from circulation – Protocol 20, line 20

Stagnation of money will not be allowed by us - Protocol 20, line 34

The people have raised a howl about the necessity of settling the question of Socialism by way of an international agreement. Division into fractional parties has given them into our hands, for, in order to carry on a contested struggle, one must have money, and the money is all in our hands. – Protocol 9, line 5

As evidenced by the above lines from 'The Protocols' the circulation of the elite's fiat currency is of the utmost importance to the continuance of their social control. That being said, it should be evident that stopping the circulation of their currency has the potential to end their false reality and reign of terror. The global shut down due to the Covid-19 release has proven this to be true, making it the easiest way to end their domination.

There are several ways we can accomplish that stagnation of currency. The most complex would be for everyone around the globe to stock up on everything needed to survive for a month, go home, and spend no more money for the rest of the month; pay no bills; BUY NOTHING; SPEND NOTHING; stay home unless you're necessary for keeping the lights on. Within a few days their fake system, propped up by deceit and make-believe will crumble and we'll be in charge. It only took a week for the elite's markets to crash when the Covid-19 "stay at home" and lock down orders went into effect.

The simplest method would be to continue with business as usual, just don't include the elite. Don't bill anybody for anything; don't collect any money; don't charge anyone for anything; essentially, just making everything free and working cooperatively will end the circulation of currency too. Whichever way we do it, and it can be discussed if/when the time comes as to how, it just has to be done in unison by all 7.8 billion of us. The elite intend to stop using money and institute a social crediting system they can control completely in a totalitarian cyber-surveillance state anyway, so the sooner we do it the better off we'll be.

The elite's only skill is the fantasy and make-believe of their false reality. They wouldn't know how to operate any of their machinations, that's what we do. We don't need them to continue on, business as usual, we're the ones in the trenches making the world turn. They'd recoil at getting their shoes dirty, let alone their hands, nor do they have the skills required to keep the world turning. We don't need them!!! Or their system!!!

"The modern banking system manufactures money out of nothing. The process is perhaps the most astounding piece of sleight-of-hand that was ever invented. Banking was conceived in inequity and born in sin. Bankers own the Earth. Take it away from them but leave them the power to create money, and with a flick of a pen, they will create enough money to buy it back again. <u>Take this great power away from them and all great fortunes like mine will disappear, for then this would be a better and happier world to live in</u>. **But if you want to continue to be the slaves of bankers and pay the cost of your own slavery, then let bankers continue to create money and control credit**." – Sir Josiah Stamp, president of the Rothschild Bank of England and the second richest man in Britain in the 1920's, speaking at the University of Texas in 1927.

"History records that the money changers have used every form of abuse, intrigue, deceit, and violent means possible to maintain their control over governments by controlling money and its issuance." – James Madison

"When a government is dependent upon bankers for money, they and not the leaders of the government control the situation, since the hand that gives is above the hand that takes…money has no motherland; financiers are without patriotism and without decency; their sole object is gain." – Napoleon Bonaparte, Emperor of France, 1815

"It is well enough that people of the nation do not understand our banking and money system, for if they did, I believe there would be a revolution before tomorrow morning." – Henry Ford, founder of the Ford Motor Company.

"From now on, depressions will be scientifically created." – Congressman Charles A. Lindbergh, on the creation of the Federal Reserve System. 1913

"The Federal Reserve Banks are one of the most corrupt institutions the world has ever seen. There is not a man within the sound of my voice who does not know that this nation is run by the international bankers." – Congressman Louis T. McFadden (Rep. – PA.)

"All problems, depressions, wars, disasters, assassinations – all of them were planned, caused, instigated, and implemented by the international bankers and their attempt to establish a central bank in every country in the world, which they have now done, thanks to corrupt politicians who have been bought and paid for. This is all you need to know about the history of the world." – Mary Elizabeth Croft

"The few who understand the system will either be so interested in its profits or be so dependent upon its favours that there will be no opposition from that class, while on the other hand, the great body of people, mentally incapable of comprehending the tremendous advantage that capital derives from the system, will bear its burdens without complaint, and perhaps without even suspecting that the system is inimical to their interests." – The Rothschild brothers of London writing to associates in New York, 1863.

Over the past 5000 years the accumulation, possession, and hoarding of gold elevated a group of ragtag usurpers, with a reputation as cutthroat bandits, possibly/probably of Sumerian origins, from homeless raiders to global elite. Along the way they infiltrated and destroyed every great civilization ever created despite being shunned and expelled from many of them multiple times.

They returned after each expulsion through devious means and connived their way into positions of influence with the leaders, resulting in the ruination of the leader and the empire. Once the bandits possessed most of the gold in the known world, they created money to continue the influence gold had given them (this history only applies to the twelve original tribes, the Ashkenazi [the thirteenth tribe] are not of the twelve tribes, they're Jewish by conversion and assimilation only).

From its creation money has been used to steal property and wealth from the people, most frequently in the form of usury (lending money at interest) among other things. The Pharisees and Sadducees generated enormous wealth with a scam they created to bilk Hebrews out of their hard-earned money with their creation, the half shekel, a silver coin. By charging admission to their temples and only accepting the half shekel as the form of payment they stole Hebrews' land, money, and lives by charging outrageous fees for the purchase of a half shekel to pay the admission into their temples to worship their imaginary god. If a Hebrew didn't have the cash, he could use his property (land, children, livestock, crops, women, etc.), or his labor, as collateral for the purchase, which, more often than not, resulted in his property, or some portion of it, being seized by the Sadducees as payment of his debt, or his becoming their slave if his life was all he had.

"THE JEWS – A PEOPLE "BORN FOR SLAVERY," AS TACITUS AND THE WHOLE ANCIENT WORLD SAY; "THE CHOSEN PEOPLE AMONG THE PEOPLE," AS THEY THEMSELVES SAY AND BELIEVE – THE JEWS HAVE BROUGHT OFF THAT MIRACULOUS FEAT OF AN INVERSION OF VALUES, THANKS TO WHICH LIFE ON EARTH HAS ACQUIRED A NOVEL AND DANGEROUS ATTRACTION FOR A COUPLE OF MILLENNIA: THEIR PROPHETS HAVE FUSED "RICH," "GODLESS," "EVIL," "VIOLENT," AND "SENSUAL" INTO ONE AND WERE THE FIRST TO USE THE WORD "WORLD" AS AN APPOROBRIUM. THIS INVERSION OF VALUES (WHICH INCLUDES USING THE WORD "POOR" AS SYNONYMOUS WITH "HOLY" AND "FRIEND") CONSTITUTES THE SIGNIFICANCE OF THE JEWISH PEOPLE: THEY MARK THE BEGINNING OF THE SLAVE REBELLION IN MORALS." – Friedrich Nietzsche, *Beyond Good and Evil: Natural History of Morals, sec. 195*

An Essenean priest from the Lebanese district of Phoenicia, Yeshua ben Joseph, was crucified as a traitor by the Roman Governor, Pontius Pilate, at the demand of The Elders of Zion for exposing their greed and corruption to the people and attempting to get them to stop worshipping at their temple and abandon their corrupt religion. For the next 2000 plus years the rule of money was insidiously spread throughout the world by the usurping hands of money-changers/bankers until it became their tool of total control it is today.

"WHO CONTROLS MONEY CONTROLS THE WORLD." – Henry Kissinger

In 1913 the financial sovereignty of the United States was sold to the Rothschilds (resulting in the Federal Reserve Bank) by the amoral and extremely corrupt president, Woodrow Wilson, for a mere $40,000 and the assurance the U.S. would continue fighting The First World War until the Rothschilds made as much money as they wanted from the conflict (even though he promised the people who elected him he'd keep them out of the war), which they instigated and backed on all sides, as they've done with every war since the 1700's. Next to usury, war is the most profitable business the Rothschilds engage in.

"IF MY SONS DID NOT WANT WARS, THERE WOULD BE NONE." –
Gutle Schnaper Rothschild

Today, all but a handful of countries have Rothschild owned central banks (a complete list of Rothschild owned central banks is provided in '*I THE PEOPLE*') and America is "at war" with those countries as I write. The fact of the matter is, the Rothschilds "own" nearly everything on the planet, either directly through a maze of complex familial ties that stretch for generations, or indirectly through their proxies, The Committee of 300, whose history dates back to the India Tea Company and The Council of 300.

Not much happens in the world that isn't a result of a whim of Lord Jacob Rothschild, the patriarch of the family and head of what conspiracy theorists have labeled "The Rothschild Banking Mafia," a who's who of the most powerful people in the world. If you've read '*I THE PEOPLE*', you know the names of every one of those people, the businesses they control, their political positions, and the councils/groups they belong to, as well as every Rothschild Central Bank in the world.

When viewed across time, it's not difficult to conclude that gold trading and money was created by the least industrious, but the most devious, in order to scam society out of its wealth, property, and power. I say that because the usury scam was created almost simultaneously with the trading of gold and money has been the bane of humankind's existence since its inception.

The hoarding of gold and money has enabled the most useless members of society to become the most powerful members of society and been the driving force in the vast majority of conflicts around the globe for thousands of years. If it wasn't rulers attempting to usurp, or steal, other rulers' wealth, it was people as greedy as the Rothschilds creating and funding both, or all, sides of a conflict for profit. Thanks to the Rothschilds' unfettered greed our cannon fodder status has been firmly entrenched in society, war has become the most profitable business on the planet, and humanity the biggest commodity.

Not only is money a cause of war, it's also the main reason the governmental systems of republics and democracies were created due to their inherent ability to be easily corrupted. There's no faster path to wealth than politics; where else can someone whose only talent is deception become a multi-millionaire in a few years on a low six-figure salary while only "working" (doing nothing but squabbling like a three-year-old) 119 days a year?

There's nothing in the world that can make or break a person's life as quickly as money, or the lack of it, nor is there anything as fickle or easy to manipulate as the economy the elite have created with their money. It's become the most important useless abstract on the planet simply because we've allowed it to and it rules every aspect of our lives and the progress mankind makes because everything hinges on the whims of the elite that control the money.

Ending the rule of money will nullify the power of the destructively useless elite and open up a world of resources that were constrained by dollar signs and the greed of the wealthy that claim to "own" them, which will allow real progress to begin. The lack of money restricts the prosperity and industry of individuals, slows or ends production, hampers research and development, and slows or stops distribution. Additionally, since the elite control all the money in the world, either directly or indirectly, they won't allow funding for anything that conflicts with their interests or they can't/won't profit from.

The want of money is also the primary cause of crime, corruption, and disparity of all sorts. What's the incentive for ninety-nine percent of the crime in this world? Money. What's the most common form of payout for corruption in governments? Money, the second being power, but power without money fades quickly, which puts money at the top of the list again, unless we're talking about an ideologically corrupt, morally bankrupt politician that will sell their mouth to the highest bidder strictly for the backing the bidder's money provides. What is "poverty?" The lack of money and advantages possession of it brings. Money is the great equalizer or oppressor depending on who possesses it and how much.

Hoarded money is the only power the bankers and the wealthy possess over society (eight people possess more wealth than half the human race combined). Eliminating money will empower everyone and make this type of societal shift only as slow as it takes for you to educate yourselves and do the work. The processes will be streamlined and quickened over time as we gain experience and knowledge of how best to adapt the technologies we're using to various environments and cultures.

It should also be noted that experts in the Artificial Intelligence realm are now stating that forty percent of the jobs humans now do will be performed by A.I. within fifteen years (ninety percent of manufacturing jobs humans once did have already been lost to automation/A.I.) and every job humans do will be performed by A.I. within no less than thirty years. However, I don't think they're taking the snowball effect into consideration here either, it seems they never do, or are they simply lying to keep people ignorant and complacent?

As A.I. learns, it also learns faster and more comprehensively and will reach a point very quickly where it can't be relegated to perform only a certain task. It will not only learn a task but it will also create a more efficient way to perform that task according to its needs not humans'. That efficiency will eliminate every income generating avenue humans now have, including creating A.I., in less than twenty years.

Wouldn't we be better off not needing an income than being totally dependent on the elite's Universal Basic Income (U.B.I.) in a social crediting system we can be locked out of at any time due to an elite's or algorithmic whim? And, how much do you think that income will be considering the elite that control the money no longer have any need for you, actually, exactly the opposite? The less of you there are the more they can keep for themselves. If you read Agenda 21, you'll find out exactly what their plan is.

END NATIONS, STATES, AND CENTRALIZED GOVERNMENTS

"THERE ARE TERRIBLE PEOPLE WHO, INSTEAD OF SOLVING A PROBLEM, BUNGLE IT AND MAKE IT MORE DIFFICULT FOR ALL WHO COME AFTER. WHOEVER CAN'T HIT THE NAIL ON THE HEAD SHOULD, PLEASE, NOT HIT IT AT ALL." – Friedrich Nietzsche, *The Wanderer and His Shadow*

"IF YOU ARE STILL ATTACHED TO YOUR RELIGION, YOUR SKIN COLOR, OR THE COUNTRY YOU WERE BORN IN, THEN YOU STILL DON'T KNOW WHO YOU ARE." – Prince Hanuman

"MADNESS IS RARE IN INDIVIDUALS – BUT IN GROUPS, PARTIES, NATIONS, AND AGES IT IS THE RULE." – Freidrich Nietzsche, *Beyond Good and Evil*

"WHEN THERE IS STATE THERE WILL BE NO FREEDOM. BUT WHEN THERE IS FREEDOM THERE WILL BE NO STATE." – Vladimir Lenin

GOVERNMENT = THE IDIOCRACY OF THE WEALTHY, BY THE WEALTHY, FOR THE WEALTHY.
THE THREE BRANCHES
FINANCIAL
PETROCHEMICAL
PHARMACEUTICAL

GOVERNMENTS CONSIST OF GREEDY, SELF-RIGHTEOUS, DELUSIONAL, AMORAL, CHILDISH, POWER-MAD, IDIOTIC, HYPOCRITICAL, EGOMANIACAL LIARS THAT BELIEVE THEY'RE ENTITLED TO DICTATE HOW OTHERS LIVE; OWNED BY PEOPLE WHO VIEW US AS CANNON FODDER OR COMMODITIES.

Nothing illustrates the preceding quote better than Nancy Pelosi being caught on camera getting her hair done at a San Francisco salon while the business was supposed to be closed due to Crovid-19 restrictions and she was supposed to be staying home, or wearing a face mask (which she wasn't) while in public. Her, "I was set up" claim and playing the victim is just the frosting on the selfish hypocritical cake that is Nancy Pelosi.

"LAW HAS BECOME A BUSINESS. HEALTHCARE HAS BECOME A BUSINESS. UNFORTUNATELY, POLITICS HAS ALSO BECOME A BUSINESS. THAT REALLY UNDERMINES SOCIETY." – George Soros

"A GOVERNMENT BIG ENOUGH TO GIVE YOU EVERYTHING YOU WANT IS BIG ENOUGH TO TAKE EVERYTHING YOU HAVE." – Paul Harvey

"WHEN YOUR ACTIONS CONTRADICT YOUR WORDS; YOUR WORDS DON'T MEAN ANYTHING." – Quentin McCall

"WHEN PEOPLE LIE TO THE GOVERNMENT IT'S A FELONY. WHEN GOVERNMENTS LIE TO THE PEOPLE IT'S POLITICS." – Bill Murray

CONGRESS IS THE OPPOSITE OF PROGRESS.

"TO PANDER TO THOSE WHO HAVE NO STOMACH FOR STRAIGHT LANGUAGE, AND INSIST UPON BLAND, NON-CONTROVERSIAL SAUCES, IS A WASTE OF TIME. THEY CANNOT OR DELIBERATELY WILL NOT UNDERSTAND WHAT WE ARE DISCUSSING." – Saul Alinsky, *Rules for Radicals*

A POLITICIAN'S MORALITY IS GOVERNED BY THE SIZE OF THEIR MASTERS' WALLETS AND WHETHER IT'S AN ELECTION YEAR OR NOT.

"POWER IS ALWAYS DANGEROUS. POWER ATTRACTS THE WORST AND CORRUPTS THE BEST." – Edward Abbey

"WHO WOULD PROTECT US IF WE DIDN'T HAVE GOVERNMENTS? THE WORLD WOULD BECOME TOTAL CHAOS." – the response from a clueless stranger when I mentioned ending governments in a conversation. Governments create chaos in order to make the people believe we need them.

EXPECTING GOVERNMENTS TO PROTECT YOU IS LIKE EXPECTING WOLVES TO PROTECT YOUR CHICKENS.

"GIVING MONEY AND POWER TO GOVERNMENT IS LIKE GIVING WHISKEY AND CAR KEYS TO TEENAGE BOYS." – P.J. O'Rourke

"MODERN POLITICS HAS BECOME LITTLE MORE THAN SHIRKING RESPONSIBILITY AND BLAMING SOMEONE ELSE." – Ross Perot

"WAR HAS RULES. MUD WRESTLING HAS RULES. POLITICS HAS NO RULES." – Ross Perot

"THERE ARE NO MORALS IN POLITICS; THERE IS ONLY EXPEDIENCE. A SCOUNDREL MAY BE OF USE TO US JUST BECAUSE HE IS A SCOUNDREL." – Vladimir Lenin

"IN OUR COUNTRY THE LIE HAS BECOME NOT JUST A MORAL CATEGORY BUT A PILLAR OF THE STATE." – Aleksandr Solzhenitsyn

"IN BUSINESS PEOPLE ARE HELD ACCOUNTABLE. IN WASHINGTON, NOBODY IS HELD ACCOUNTABLE. IN BUSINESS, PEOPLE ARE JUDGED ON RESULTS. IN WASHINGTON PEOPLE ARE MEASURED BY THEIR ABILITY TO GET RE-ELECTED." – Ross Perot

Although Nietzsche was referencing the hypocrisy of religion and its "holy men" in the following quote I found that it reminded me more of politicians than priests, so I decided to use it here. I'm sure Nietzsche wouldn't mind, he thought no more of politicians and governments than priests.

"WHY STROKE THE EFFEMINATE EARS OF OUR MODERN WEAKLINGS? WHY SHOULD *WE* GIVE WAY EVEN ONE STEP TO THEIR TARTUFFERY (**hypocrisy, pharisaism, phoniness**) OF WORDS? FOR US PSYCHOLOGISTS THIS WOULD CONSTITUTE A TARTUFFERY IN *DEED,* QUITE APART FROM THE FACT THAT IT WOULD NAUSEATE US. FOR IF A PSYCHOLOGIST TODAY HAS *GOOD TASTE* (OTHERS MIGHT SAY, INTEGRITY) IT CONSISTS IN RESISTANCE TO THE SHAMEFULLY *MORALIZED* WAY OF SPEAKING WHICH HAS

GRADUALLY MADE ALL MODERN JUDGEMENTS OF MEN AND THINGS SLIMY." – Freidrich Neitzsche, *On the Genealogy of Morals*

Large centralized governments arose as a byproduct of the shift from small hunter-gatherer societies that laid no claim to the land and roamed it freely to commercial agriculturally based permanent city-states and eventually empires lorded over by god-kings and emperors.

Governments initially arose as a body tasked with enforcing the rulers' edicts whose primary job was to capitulate and proliferate wars, either for protection from those the ruler deemed a threat or to steal their territory and exterminate and/or subjugate them. Almost as an afterthought it also became the government's bailiwick to see to the needs of the people (without people there would be no army), which was why representative types of government were formed.

In the earliest forms of empires and nation-states it was impossible to convey the needs of all the people to a centralized location (the capitol) in a timely manner. Therefore, representatives of districts or regions were sent to the capitol to voice the needs of their neighbors/constituents. Enter rampant corruption, once away from their home-turf those representatives were easily influenced to adhere to the elite's agendas with special favors, often and primarily involving bribery with gold or money, property or goods, power, or a combination thereof.

"FOR THE GOOD – THEY *CANNOT* CREATE: THEY ARE ALWAYS THE BEGINNING OF THE END: – THEY CRUCIFY HIM WHO WRITES NEW VALUES ON A NEW TABLET, THEY SACRIFICE THE FUTURE *TO THEMSELVES* – THEY CRUCIFY THE WHOLE HUMAN FUTURE!" – Freidrich Nietzsche, *Thus Spoke Zarathustra*

Both republics and democracies (except for the Iroquois Democracy, which was designed to thwart corruption and war. Initially the founding fathers modeled their government after the Iroquois Confederacy but it was perverted into a Roman Republic long ago) were created for one specific reason…they gave the illusion of being "for the people" while being the easiest to corrupt.

Today's representatives now dictate to the people what they want them to want and believe, whether they want or need it, or believe it or not, such as Barack Obama and Nancy Pelosi telling Americans, "that's not who we are" to further their socialist agenda or Donald Trump telling Americans they want a border wall for their safety and putting millions of Americans in harm's way by shutting down the government in a failed attempt to get his way.

Selfishness, ideological and financial corruption, juvenile squabbling, name calling, and finger pointing (the blame game) has become the stock in trade of modern governments, now a tug-of-war between socialists and corporatists with ignorant, propagandized citizens caught in the middle cheering for one side or the other without even knowing, or caring to know, what they're actually cheering for. All they know is their favorite puppet told them what they want and they're for it, especially when the economy's booming and there are plenty of jobs.

Little do they realize; economy is the enemy of humanity and a major driving force behind all the environmental and societal ills we face today. Nor do they understand, it's the bankers that really regulate the economy and their lobbyists that make the laws, not the politicians, politicians are just the front men that tell you what they want you to want or what they think you want to hear so you won't rebel against the lobbyists' laws. It's all part of a much larger plan that caters to the elite encompassing the globe, what the people want or need is immaterial. We're given just enough to keep us from outright total rebellion and refusal to continue following the elite's whims.

Do we really need a group of ideologically and financially corrupt, morally bankrupt idiots whose only forte is drama and propaganda dictating how we should think and live because it benefits them far more than us? I don't think so and if you knew more than how to get to work, do your job, provide the proper knee-jerk reaction to your favorite puppet's rhetoric, and your favorite TV shows, or sports stats, you wouldn't either.

This archaic representative type of centralized government we have is entirely unnecessary in this age of instant connection. Local government is all that's needed for our day to day existence. For larger issues in a connected intelligent society all we need is a news reader to present the issue to the people over the television and within forty-eight to seventy-two hours everyone's voice could be heard via the internet, a consensus established, a plan of action created, and ratification by the population or another plan formulated if necessary, for the satisfaction of all. This is just a rough introduction to this idea, there will be much more refinement later in this work.

PREACHERS AND POLITICIANS ARE NOTHING MORE THAN WORLD-CLASS SNAKE OIL SALESMEN. THE WORLD WOULD BE A MUCH

BETTER PLACE WITHOUT THEM AND THE INSTITUTIONS THEY
REPRESENT.

AS THE WORLD BURNS
DUMBER VS DUMBEST
Who's who is anybody's guess.
"THINK OF HOW STUPID THE AVERAGE PERSON IS, AND THEN
REALIZE HALF OF THEM ARE STUPIDER THAN THAT." – George
Carlin

STUPID PEOPLE ELECT STUPIDER POLITICIANS

"IF YOU HAVE SELFISH, IGNORANT CITIZENS, YOU'RE GONNA
HAVE SELFISH, IGNORANT LEADERS." – George Carlin

It's that time again. Time to choose the **lesser of two evils** and which
idiot's lies you're dumb enough to believe; the most common form of
Controlled Opposition used in general elections today. **Utopian dreamer**
being the most common form of Controlled Opposition used during the
primaries.

ALLOWING YOURSELF TO BE LED ALLOWS YOU TO BE MISLEAD

TRUMP:
Toddler on a sugar rush.
"IF YOU TELL A LIE BIG ENOUGH AND KEEP REPEATING IT, PEOPLE
WILL EVENTUALLY COME TO BELIEVE IT." – Joseph Goebbels, Nazi
Propaganda Minister

DONALD TRUMP'S PROOF POSITIVE THAT IGNORANCE AND
STUPIDITY ARE THE TWO MOST DANGEROUS THINGS IN THE
WORLD.

Will it be the lies (nearly 70,000 to date) of a well-known narcissistic,
delusionary, egomaniacal, attention craving, unprincipled pathologically
lying, hyper-corrupt corporatist that has no concept of reality, facts, or
science while claiming to know everything. A poor little rich kid who's
only concerned with himself, his reelection, making his cronies
wealthier, and bragging about an economy built on the backs of taxing
"his people" (the less one makes the more they're taxed, with those

making the least being taxed the most) while giving his billionaire cronies massive tax breaks and pardoning people that kiss his ignorant ass. A self-absorbed clown that's laughable to other leaders who know by stroking his ego he can be played like a fiddle and disparagingly accuses his opponents of planning to do the same things they accuse him of planning to do, or is doing (a world champion blame game player).

A wannabe 'dictator' of sorts (as evidenced by the hard looks he gives journalists as he lies right to their faces during press conferences, as if he's daring them to continue exposing his lie[s].), that sycophantically idolizes strong man dictators like Putin, Xi, Kim, Erdogan, and Bolsonaro and does all he can to emulate them. For example, dividing the population via racial, ideological, and economic disparities; using those divisions to create social chaos; then sending in federal troops to escalate the violence and claiming he's the only one that can "protect" society from the chaos he created – a classic tactic of every dictator throughout history that's currently in use by Jair Bolsonaro in Brazil, Nicolas Maduro in Venezuela, Recep Erdogan in Turkey, and Alexander Lukashenko in Belarus.

Trump's "leadership" style is as simple as his voters – ignore and/or deny problems unless he's being impugned, then he lies about everything; blame others for the problems and fires them when lying and juvenile name-calling doesn't work; brags that he's doing a fantastic job, and shamelessly promotes himself as brilliant while being anything but.

In his infinitely delusionary and idiotic mind Trump has now hit on what he considers a foolproof plan to rig the election in his favor. There's been a push for mail-in voting due to the pandemic for months. Trump has claimed repeatedly that it's a socialist conspiracy to rig the election in their favor and refuses to allow it claiming it's too easy to corrupt and we may never know the results, even though he's voted by mail the last two elections and made the usual self-aggrandizing show of filling out his mail-in ballot for this election while his campaign mailed out mail-in ballot request forms to all registered voters.

He's also ended the in-person security briefings to congress claiming they've been found to leak info to whomever it concerns. And, he's now telling everyone to send in their mail-in ballot, check on its status on election day, and vote again in-person if it hasn't been counted yet. Effectively, telling everyone to vote twice, which is illegal.

In order to totally confound their "plan" Trump's now appointed one of his wealthy idiot cronies, Louis DeJoy, a heavily invested competitor ($30 to $75million in XPO Logistics, J.B. Hunt, and UPS) of the U.S.P.S. as Postmaster General, to dismantle and gut the postal system in order to slow it down to a crawl, if not stop it (harming countless Americans, especially the elderly, who depend on the post office's timely delivery of medications and other necessities). He decided he'd defund the post office in order to force voters to go to the polls in person, hoping it will suppress voter turnout due to fears of spreading/contracting Covid-19, especially at-risk voters. He's threatened to contest the election because he believes that the only way he can lose is if the Democrats/socialists succeed in rigging it.

Trump's tartuffery abounds; today, 8/29/2020, I received a mail-in ballot request form from the Trump campaign in the mail.

The man who would be dictator, Donald J. Trump, is a legend in his own mind.

- He's a failure as a businessman. Trump's businesses have filed bankruptcy six times, leaving employees and creditors in the lurch. His fraudulent "university" was sued by attendees for providing nothing and shut down. He's destroyed natural spaces to build golf courses and attempted to stop clean energy projects that were near them. He's lost more money than he's made and he constantly inflates his worth to appear more successful than he really is. His credit is so bad that only Russian oligarchs will work with him, which explains his sycophantic behavior toward Putin.
  "Russians make up a pretty disproportionate cross-section of a lot of our assets" – Donald Trump JR, 2008
  "We don't rely on American banks. We have all the funding we need out of Russia." – Donald Trump JR, 2014
- He's a failure as a president. His "great" economy is built on the destruction of aquifers, natural parks, forests, and monuments, and the use of the dirtiest sources of energy. He justifies this by claiming he "doesn't believe in climate change, it's a Chinese hoax created to end American manufacturing." He's given his billionaire cronies massive tax cuts while increasing taxes on the working class and the poor, with the poor paying the most per dollar earned. He listens to no one, believes he knows everything, and claims whatever he doesn't agree with is a hoax, or that someone's out to make him look bad, something he does very well all by himself. His presidency is just a surreal unreality show played out daily on Twitter and in the media. He "handles" issues by either ignoring them, denying them, lying about them, blaming someone else, or firing someone. He ignores or

denies facts and science and discredits scientists and those who adhere to them, while he claims to know more than anyone else about everything and does nothing but lie and deny, i.e. Covid-19 will "magically disappear" (especially when they stop testing for it) and/or "it's going away" while it worsens daily because he's forcing schools to open and people to go back to work prematurely. He's handling the protests of law enforcements' shootings and murders of Black Americans by sending the National Guard into cities with the result of escalating the violence, not quelling it. On 8/8/2020 Trump announced he will defer the payroll tax that funds Social Security and Medicare until the end of the year and if reelected will end it permanently, effectively ending the income and medical insurance for 65 million American senior citizens. He's doing this due to his feeble response to Covid-19 and his subsequent refusal to fund another stimulus package because he'd rather force people back to work and children back to school. Which is backfiring as infection and death rates skyrocket.

- Worst of all, he's a failure as a human being. He only cares about himself and what's good for him. This sometimes leads people to believe he has some sort of empathy when he displays a caring manner, but his caring is only a show for someone he thinks may be able to do something for him, or has done something for him, it doesn't extend to the entire population. As far as you and I go, he could care less, especially if you're a woman, unless he gets called to the carpet. Then, he says, or tweets, something stupid and callous and moves on. He holds Americans', especially seniors', well-being hostage in a yet unsuccessful attempt to coerce the socialists in congress to give him what he wants. His recent move to defund Social Security and Medicare by deferring the payroll tax that funds them has proven beyond a shadow of a doubt that he could care less about senior citizens. It indicates he's either serious about extending the federal unemployment benefits the socialists refused to consider unless they got their way or he intends to hold seniors hostage for leverage once again in order to get the socialists to lower their stimulus package demands to the billion dollars he agreed to.

Trump's failure is so egregious that staunch republicans, especially those that worked closely with him, are turning to Biden in hopes he can repair at least some of the damage Trump's self-serving egomaniacal actions have wrought. They're gonna regret that too, Biden's nothing more than the socialists' stocking horse and will just be a corrupt and more radical Obamaist. Which leads me to say something "positive." Trump's not in it to steal money, he's in it for the attention and will get it any way he can, whether it's positive or negative.

The Republican National Convention spent four nights attempting to normalize Trump's incessant lying, denying, ignoring, juvenile name-calling, self-absorption, and tweeting by claiming he was "doing it his own way," and painting him as a great humanitarian. Mike Pence stated Trump wasn't a politician, he was a leader that got the job done no matter what he had to do to accomplish it. A constant parade of women, including a nun, sang the praises of Trump in an effort to neutralize the ongoing effect of the Access Hollywood Interview. His family members, especially his children and their spouses, attempted to portray the family as being 'as American as apple pie' while they were driven to the best private schools in limousines and wanted for nothing. As with the D.N.C. the tartuffery overflowed.

On the plus side, Trump's done more for America and Americans in four years than all but a few politicians, especially Joe Biden, have done in their entire career. Your average politician makes a lot of grand promises during their campaign, does nothing during their term if elected, blames someone else for doing nothing and reiterates the same promises when they run for reelection. Despite all his myriad of faults Trump did as much as he could do to fulfill his promises with an obstructionist congress thwarting his every move.

September 9th, 2020, Trump was nominated for the Nobel Peace Prize today due to his involvement in brokering a peace deal between Israel and U.A.E. and Bahrain, even though they weren't engaged in any conflict. He's even doing things he never mentioned in his 2016 campaign.

September 10th, 2020, Trump finally admitted to lying to Americans about the Covid-19 pandemic, of course immediately afterward he deflected blame to Bob Woodward and claimed Jonathan Karl asked a "terrible question" when he asked why he lied to the people and said "I didn't lie."

BIDEN:
Beijing Biden

"THE MORE THINGS CHANGE, THE MORE THEY REMAIN THE SAME." – Jean-Baptiste Alphonse Karr

ANY MAN ENDORSED BY LIARS, THIEVES, SEXUAL PREDITORS, HYPOCRITES, AND THE CORRUPT MUST ALSO BE A LIAR, THIEF, SEXUAL PREDITOR, HYPOCRITE, AND CORRUPT.

"GOOD MEN NEVER SPEAK THE TRUTH." – Freidrich Nietzsche, *Thus Spoke Zarathustra, On old and New Tablets, sec. 7*

Or, will it be a do-nothing, lying, career politician, whose only real successful political experience is opening his mouth and inserting his foot up to the knee, groping/inappropriately touching women, apologizing for it when caught, and syphoning taxpayer money into family members' bank accounts and businesses. A career hypocrite, chameleon, socialist, and plagiarist (regularly stealing other politicians' speeches, with Trump's "America First" motto being his most recent plagiarism) who's never had an original thought, that says what he thinks you want to hear, and does as much nothing as he possibly can by way of follow through while blaming others for his shortcomings and riding others' coattails. A professional shirker and excuse maker that couldn't lead a group of children to the restroom.

It's definitely worth noting that Biden's current campaign platform is exactly the opposite of his politics during his entire forty-seven-year always-do-the-wrong-thing political career with lining his and his family's pockets with ill-gotten money being his greatest talent.

In all fairness, I must say that Biden does come from a working-class background and brings an appearance of that humanity to his work and campaign as best he can, whereas Trump was born with a golden spoon in his mouth, doesn't have an ounce of empathy or compassion for anything or anyone, only thinks of himself, and has turned his presidency into a self-aggrandizing unreality show with his incessant idiotic tweeting and constant chaotic hypocritical lying about absolutely everything.

Well, it's no longer a secret. Mister do-nothing's found a perfect do-nothing as his running mate, Kamala Harris. The media's calling his decision "historic" because Harris is the first Indian/Jamaican woman to be selected as a vice-presidential running mate. I think it's historic because the level of waffling mendacity has just gone off the charts and this "election" will be nothing more than a meeting of the Liars Club to see who can make the biggest claims and promises and not only fail to follow through on any of them, but radically expedite an already rapidly declining society.

"OH MY BROTHERS! WITH WHOM LIES THE GREATEST DANGER TO THE WHOLE HUMAN FUTURE? IS IT NOT WITH THE GOOD AND JUST? – WITH THOSE WHO SAY AND FEEL IN THEIR HEARTS: "WE ALREADY KNOW WHAT IS GOOD AND JUST, WE HAVE IT TOO: WOE TO THOSE WHO ARE STILL SEARCHING FOR IT! AND WHATEVER HARM THE EVIL MAY DO, THE HARM THE GOOD DO IS THE MOST HARMFUL HARM." – Freidrich Nietzsche, *Thus Spoke Zarathustra*

IT'S BEEN MY EXPERIENCE THAT PEOPLE ARE THE EXACT OPPOSITE OF WHAT THEY CLAIM TO BE, ESPECIALLY THOSE SEEKING PUBLIC OFFICE, BE IT PRESIDENT OR DOGCATCHER.

The media would have you believe that Biden and Harris "pulled no punches" during the Democratic National Convention. Of course they didn't, there were no serious punches thrown. The bulk of the convention was convincing voters that Biden was a decent guy that believed in god, family, and country and was as honest as the day is long. If you've followed politics and dug into the backgrounds of those that would be your "leaders" as long as I have, you know it's the "decent, god-fearing, family men" that have the most skeletons in their closets, and Joe Biden is no exception, in fact he's the rule.

Here's my experience with some "decent guys." Many years ago, I regularly hauled meat from the Midwest to a distributor in the Brooklyn, New York, Bowery, an area that was even more dangerous than Hunt's Point Market. They wanted us there at 5am, which means driving a semi load of meat through the worst parts of New York City in the middle of the night and parking on the side of the street until they opened. Something many truck drivers would consider insane and absolutely refuse to do and I did the first time I was dispatched there. Instead I got there at 7:30am when people were out and about and it was daylight.

It was impossible to miss the identical gold on gold with gold appointments Cadillacs parked in front of the offices as I walked into the warehouse to turn in my bills. They had "Wise Guys" (Made Men) written all over them. The dock foreman just pointed to a door when I tried to lay my bills on his podium. The well-dressed man in the office on the other side of the door glanced at my bills quickly and asked why I was late. I told him I didn't like the idea of driving through or parking in the Bowery late at night. He looked at me for a long second then said, "come with me."

Back out on the sidewalk he had me look up and down the street in the block we were on and up to the next block. The block where we stood was free of graffiti, the street was clean, and the buildings were obviously well maintained. The next block up was covered in graffiti. People and trash were everywhere and the rundown buildings' stoops were full of people hanging out and partying. He said, "that goes on 24/7 on that block but not down here. This block is always clean and safe. You can sleep all night in your truck with both doors hanging wide open and no one, not even a hooker, will bother you. Don't ever be late again. In fact, if you get here early, we'll see to it that you get out early enough to get to your next stop in Jersey before the traffic starts. If you want anything, girls, dope, food, anything, just call the number on your bills and it'll be here when you get here, got it?" I got it.

They turned out to be the best place to deliver to in all of New York City. You never broke down your pallets, they had lumpers that did it for you. On Monday mornings they bought pizza for everybody and true to their word, they made sure anything you wanted was waiting for you when you set your brakes at their curb. They always asked how you were doing and if you needed anything. If you did, they found something you could do, like taking a short pallet of product, or an envelope of paperwork, to your next stop for them and paid handsomely for it. They were decent guys that took care of those that took care of them, but at the end of the day they were Made Men that didn't get that way by being Boy Scouts. Being a great family man or a decent guy doesn't necessarily mean you're a good and decent politician.

ACTIONS SPEAK LOUDER THAN WORDS
JOE BIDEN HAS BEEN ON THE WRONG SIDE OF EVERY ISSUE HIS ENTIRE POLITICAL CAREER.
"JOE DOESN'T LIE" – the Obamas, the Clintons, Al Gore and testimonials from family members
"Come on man, look at my record" – Joe Biden
LET'S DO JUST THAT

During the DNC some of the greatest most corrupt liars on record, the Clintons, the Obamas, and Al Gore claimed Biden is honest to a fault and never lies.

The following information and so much more can be found here: https://www.unsuited.org/?utm_source=google&utm_medium=search&utm_campaign=unsuited_pennsylvania&utm_content=name_id&gclid=EAIaIQobChMI1NSk9eWq6wIVCTiGCh3sCQKFEAAYASAAEgKxQvD_BwE

Here are some of a few of his most prominent lies:
- He said his helicopter was "forced down" near Osama bin Laden's lair in Afghanistan. His helicopter landed due to a snow storm and he was taken to an American airbase till his tour could resume.
- He said he was a coal miner. No one in his family ever got near a coal mine.
- He said he was "shot at" in Iraq. A mortar exploded a few hundred yards from his hotel in the Green Zone of Bagdad.
- He said he participated in sit-ins at segregated restaurants and movie theaters. A Black member of his high school football team was refused service in a restaurant; Biden knew nothing about it until much later and did nothing.
- During his 1988 campaign, with much pomposity, Biden told New Hampshire voters he attended Syracuse University College of Law on a full scholarship, graduated at the top of his class with three degrees, and won an outstanding student award in political science. The truth is he went on a half scholarship, never won any awards, and graduated at the bottom of his class with one degree.
- "I didn't say that" is his usual lie when caught in a lie, which is often.

A couple days after his lies about college were exposed, he ended his campaign.

Biden was a pivotal figure in Obama's "Spygate" scandal during the 2016 election, which involved administration officials illegally targeting and spying on Trump, his campaign and its officials, his associates, and General Michael Flynn. Flynn, Trump's National Security Advisor was targeted and "set up" by Obama's henchmen in an effort to get him to lie so he could be caught, prosecuted, and fired. The case was dropped by the DOJ when it concluded that Flynn was set up. When asked about his role in Flynn's being set up and the ensuing illegal investigation Biden stated, "I know NOTHING about those moves to investigate Michael Flynn" and that he "was aware that there was – that they asked for an investigation, but that's all I know about it and I don't think anything else," in spite of being present when the scheme was cooked up.

Those lies were directly contradicted by FBI agent Peter Strozk's notes, which laid out the following:
- James Comey personally knew that Flynn's actions were legal.
- President Obama ordered the FBI to investigate Flynn anyway.

- Joe Biden was actively involved in the investigation and suggested things he thought they could prosecute Flynn with.

Biden claimed he was an unknowing bystander in an attempt to conceal his involvement in Spygate, but it's abundantly evident he was a key player in the plot.

Sources:

The Michael Flynn Case

FBI Records Unsealed

Senate Judiciary Information

"JOE'S HONEST" – Every testimonial during the DNC

UKRAINE

In 2014, Joe Biden's lobbyist son Hunter was given a board position with the company Burisma, which is one of the largest gas companies in the Ukraine. While Joe Biden was vice president and the Obama administration's main figure on all matters related to the Ukraine; Hunter Biden was receiving $50,000 dollars or more month for this position. Eventually, Burisma came under investigation by the Ukrainian government for corruption.

In 2016, Joe Biden then blackmailed Ukrainian Prime Minister Petro Poroshenko into firing the prosecutor who was investigating Burisma. He threatened to withhold a billion dollars in US aid money unless he fired the prosecutor. The prosecutor, Viktor Shokin, was fired.

Joe Biden then bragged about having the prosecutor fired at a foreign policy event. "I said, 'You're not getting the billion.' I'm going to be leaving here in, I think it was about six hours. I looked at them and said: 'I'm leaving in six hours. If the prosecutor is not fired, you're not getting the money,'" Biden recalled telling Poroshenko.

"Well, son of a bitch, he got fired. And they put in place someone who was solid at the time." – Joe Biden at the Council on Foreign Relations.

Hunter Biden stayed on Burisma's board earning at least $600,000 a year until last year.

Sources:

Biden Brags About Getting Prosecutor Fired

Joe Biden Under Probe

Hunter Biden Payout Far Above Others

Joe Biden's 2020 Nightmare - A Probe Revived

BIDEN LINKED INVESTMENT GROUP FUNDED CHINESE MILITARY PROXY GUILTY OF STEALING AMERICAN NUCLEAR TECHNOLOGY

"An investment firm directed by Democrat presidential candidate Joe Biden's son Hunter funneled millions into China General Nuclear Power

Corp, a state-owned power company guilty of stealing American nuclear technology for use by the Chinese Communist Party for decades." – The National Pulse

JOE BIDEN HAS ENRICHED MANY OF HIS FAMILY MEMBERS

The following information about Biden's influence in attaining large amounts of money for his family is laid out in a New York Post article from author Peter Schweizer. Below is the article:

Peter Schweizer | January 18, 2020

"Political figures have long used their families to route power and benefits for their own self-enrichment. In my new book, "Profiles in Corruption: Abuse of Power by America's Progressive Elite," one particular politician — Joe Biden — emerges as the king of the sweetheart deal, with no less than five family members benefiting from his largesse, favorable access and powerful position for commercial gain. In Biden's case, these deals include foreign partners and, in some cases, even US taxpayer dollars.

The Biden family's apparent self-enrichment involves five family members: Joe's son Hunter, son-in-law Howard, brothers James and Frank, and sister Valerie.

When this subject came up in 2019, Biden declared, "I never talked with my son or my brother or anyone else — even distant family — about their business interests. Period."

As we will see, this is far from the case ...

James Biden

Joe Biden's younger brother, James, has been an integral part of the family political machine from the earliest days when he served as finance chair of Joe's 1972 Senate campaign, and the two have remained quite close. After Joe joined the US Senate, he would bring his brother James along on congressional delegation trips to places like Ireland, Rome and Africa.

When Joe became vice president, James was a welcomed guest at the White House, securing invitations to such important functions as a state dinner in 2011 and the visit of Pope Francis in 2015. Sometimes, James' White House visits dovetailed with his overseas business dealings, and his commercial opportunities flourished during his brother's tenure as vice president.

Consider the case of HillStone International, a subsidiary of the huge construction management firm Hill International. The president of HillStone International was Kevin Justice, who grew up in Delaware and was a longtime Biden family friend. On Nov. 4, 2010, according to White

House visitors' logs, Justice visited the White House and met with Biden adviser Michele Smith in the Office of the Vice President.

Less than three weeks later, HillStone announced that James Biden would be joining the firm as an executive vice president. James appeared to have little or no background in housing construction, but that did not seem to matter to HillStone. His bio on the company's website noted his "40 years of experience dealing with principals in business, political, legal and financial circles across the nation and internationally..."

James Biden was joining HillStone just as the firm was starting negotiations to win a massive contract in war-torn Iraq. Six months later, the firm announced a contract to build 100,000 homes. It was part of a $35 billion, 500,000-unit project deal won by TRAC Development, a South Korean company. HillStone also received a $22 million US federal government contract to manage a construction project for the State Department.

David Richter, son of the parent company's founder, was not shy in explaining HillStone's success in securing government contracts. It really helps, he told investors at a private meeting, to have "the brother of the vice president as a partner," according to someone who was there.

The Iraq project was massive, perhaps the single most lucrative project for the firm ever. In 2012, Charlie Gasparino of Fox Business reported that HillStone officials expected the project to "generate $1.5 billion in revenues over the next three years." That amounted to more than three times the revenue the company produced in 2011.

A group of minority partners, including James Biden, stood to split about $735 million. "There's plenty of money for everyone if this project goes through," said one company official.

The deal was all set, but HillStone made a crucial error. In 2013, the firm was forced to back out of the contract because of a series of problems, including a lack of experience by Hill and TRAC Development, its South Korean associate firm. But HillStone continued doing significant contract work in the embattled country, including a six-year contract with the US Army Corps of Engineers.

James Biden remained with Hill International, which accumulated contracts from the federal government for dozens of projects, including projects in the United States, Puerto Rico, Mozambique and elsewhere.

Hunter Biden

With the election of his father as vice president, Hunter Biden launched businesses fused to his father's power that led him to lucrative deals with a rogue's gallery of governments and oligarchs around the world. Sometimes he would hitch a prominent ride with his father aboard Air Force Two to visit a country where he was courting business. Other times, the deals would be done more discreetly. Always they involved foreign entities that appeared to be seeking something from his father.

There was, for example, Hunter's involvement with an entity called Burnham Financial Group, where his business partner Devon Archer — who'd been at Yale with Hunter — sat on the board of directors. Burnham became the vehicle for a number of murky deals abroad, involving connected oligarchs in Kazakhstan and state-owned businesses in China. But one of the most troubling Burnham ventures was here in the United States, in which Burnham became the center of a federal investigation involving a $60 million fraud scheme against one of the poorest Indian tribes in America, the Oglala Sioux.

Devon Archer was arrested in New York in May 2016 and charged with "orchestrating a scheme to defraud investors and a Native American tribal entity of tens of millions of dollars." Other victims of the fraud included several public and union pension plans. Although Hunter Biden was not charged in the case, his fingerprints were all over Burnham. The "legitimacy" that his name and political status as the vice president's son lent to the plan was brought up repeatedly in the trial.

The scheme was explicitly designed to target pension funds that had "socially responsible investing" clauses, including pension funds of labor union organizations that had publicly supported Joe Biden's political campaigns in the past. Indeed, eight of the 11 pension funds that lost their money were either government employee or labor union pension funds. Joe Biden has "a long-standing alliance with labor." He closely identifies with organized labor. "I make no apologies," he has said. "I am a union man, period." And many public unions have endorsed him over the years.

Transcripts from Archer's trial offer a clearer picture of Hunter Biden's role at Burnham Asset Management, in particular, the fact that the firm relied on his father's name and political status as a means of both recruiting pension money into the scheme and alleviating investors' concerns.

Tim Anderson, a lawyer who did legal work on the issuance of the tribal bonds, recounts seeing Hunter while visiting the Burnham office in New York City to meet with Bevan Cooney, who was later convicted in the case.

The political ties that Biden and Archer had were considered key to the Burnham brand. As stated in an August 2014 email, Jason Galanis, who was convicted in the bond scheme, agreed with an unidentified associate who also thought the company had "value beyond capital" because of their political connections.

In the closing arguments at the trial, one of Archer's defense attorneys, Matthew Schwartz, explained to the jury that it was impossible to talk about the bond scheme without mentioning Hunter Biden's name. This "was perfectly sensible," according to Schwartz, "because Hunter Biden was part of the Burnham team."

Howard Krein

It would be a dream for any new company to announce their launch in the Oval Office at 1600 Pennsylvania Avenue. StartUp Health is an investment consultancy based out of New York City, and in June 2011, the company barely had a website. The firm was the brainchild of three siblings from Philadelphia. Steven Krein is CEO and co-founder, while his brother, Dr. Howard Krein, serves as chief medical officer. Sister Bari serves as the firm's chief strategy officer. A friend named Unity Stoakes is a co-founder and serves as president.

StartUp Health was barely up and running when, in June 2011, two of the company's executives were ushered into the Oval Office of the White House. They met with President Barack Obama and Vice President Joe Biden. The following day, the new company would be featured at a large health care tech conference being run by the US Department of Health and Human Services, and StartUp Health executives became regular visitors to the White House, attending events in 2011, 2014 and 2015.

How did StartUp Health gain access to the highest levels of power in Washington? There was nothing particularly unique about the company, but for this: The chief medical officer of StartUp Health, Howard Krein, is married to Joe Biden's youngest daughter, Ashley. "I happened to be talking to my father-in-law that day and I mentioned Steve and Unity were down there [in Washington, DC]," recalled Howard Krein. "He knew about StartUp Health and was a big fan of it. He asked for Steve's number and said, 'I have to get them up here to talk with Barack.' The Secret Service came and got Steve and Unity and brought them to the Oval Office."

StartUp Health offers to provide new companies technical and relationship advice in exchange for a stake in the business. Demonstrating and highlighting the fact that you can score a meeting with the president of the United States certainly helps prove a strategic company asset: high-level contacts.

Vice President Joe Biden continued to help Krein promote his company at several appearances through his last months in the White House, including one in January 2017, where he made a surprise showing at the StartUp Health Festival in San Francisco. The corporate event, open only to StartUp Health members, enabled the 250 people in attendance to chat in a closed session with the vice president.

Frank Biden

In late March 2009, Vice President Joe Biden landed in Costa Rica aboard Air Force Two, and went to the Costa Rican presidential palace for a one-on-one with President Oscar Arias. The Biden visit had symbolic significance. The last time a high-ranking American official had visited the country was back in 1997, when Bill Clinton had come.

Joe Biden's trip to Costa Rica came at a fortuitous time for his brother Frank, who was busy working deals in the country. Just months after Vice President Biden's visit, in August, Costa Rica News announced a new multilateral partnership "to reform Real Estate in Latin America" among Frank Biden, a developer named Craig Williamson, and the Guanacaste Country Club, a newly planned resort. The partnership, which appears to be ongoing, was wrapped in a beautiful package as a "call on resources available to the companies and individuals to reform the social, economic and environmental practices of real estate developers across the world by example."

In real terms, Frank's dream was to build in the jungles of Costa Rica thousands of homes, a world-class golf course, casinos, and an anti-aging center. The Costa Rican government was eager to cooperate with the vice president's brother. As it happened, Joe Biden had been asked by President Obama to act as the administration's point man in Latin America and the Caribbean.

Frank's vision for a country club in Costa Rica received support from the highest levels of the Costa Rican government — despite his lack of experience in building such developments. He met with the Costa Rican ministers of education and energy and environment, as well as the president of the country.

On Oct. 4, 2016, the Costa Rican Ministry of Public Education signed a letter of intent with Frank's company, Sun Fund Americas. The project involved allowing a company called GoSolar to operate solar power facilities in Costa Rica. The previous year, the Obama-Biden administration's OPIC had authorized a $6.5 million taxpayer-backed loan for the project.

In June 2014, Vice President Biden announced the launch of the Caribbean Energy Security Initiative (CESI). The program called for increasing access to financing for Caribbean energy projects that he strongly supported. American taxpayer dollars were dedicated to facilitating deals that matched US government financing with local *energy projects in Caribbean countries, including Jamaica. In January 2015, USAID announced that it would be spending $10 million to boost renewable energy projects in Jamaica over the next five years.*

After Joe Biden brought together leaders for CESI, brother Frank's firm Sun Fund Americas announced that it was "engaged in projects and is in negotiations with governments of other countries in the [Caribbean] region for both its Solar and Waste to Energy development services." As if to push the idea along, the Obama administration's OPIC provided a $47.5 million loan to support the construction of a 20-megawatt solar facility in Clarendon, Jamaica.

Frank Biden's Sun Fund Americas later announced that it had signed a power purchase agreement to build a 20-megawatt solar facility in Jamaica.

Valerie Biden Owens

During his years in the Senate, Biden's family benefited financially in other ways as he leveraged political power. Joe's sister Valerie ran all of his Senate campaigns, as well as his presidential runs in 1988 and 2008. But she was also a senior partner in a political messaging firm named Joe Slade White & Company; the only two executives listed at the firm were Joe Slade White and Valerie.

The firm received large fees from the Biden campaigns that Valerie was running. Two and a half million dollars in consulting fees flowed to her firm from Citizens for Biden and Biden For President Inc. during the 2008 presidential bid alone. Joe Slade White & Company worked for Biden campaigns over 18 years."

FBI INVESTIGATED JOE BIDEN'S CAMPAIGN FOR ILLEGAL CAMPAIGN FUNDING

"Christopher Tigani was a wealthy beer distributor who relished his close ties to Delaware politicians, particularly Joe Biden, when the FBI confronted him outside a Royal Farms gas station in September 2010. Tigani was in trouble. While serving as a bundler for Biden's aborted 2008 presidential campaign, he had reimbursed his employees for contributions made in their names, a well-worn tactic for circumventing campaign-finance laws.

What happened between that day and Tigani's 2012 sentencing has never before been revealed: He would wear a wire for the FBI and record people close to the then-vice president, seeking, he said, to confirm his belief that they knew of his reimbursements and investigate whether they, or others close to Biden, engaged in any quid pro quo deals with donors.

Over several months in 2011, Tigani said, his handlers used him to try to elicit cooperation from others closer to the then-vice president and even discussed trying to get him in front of Biden himself while wearing a wire. Tigani said he recorded conversations with former Biden finance chief Dennis Toner as well as a businessman close to Biden and a Biden aide-turned-lobbyist. He said he also sought to develop evidence against other players in Delaware politics." – Politico

MR. TOUCHY-FEELY
Joe Biden has a documented history of inappropriate and abhorrent behavior with women. His actions often occur during high-profile and ceremonial events. This article documents FORTY instances of this behavior: https://cloverchronicle.com/2019/04/29/video-collection-here-are-40-reasons-why-joe-biden-the-open-sexual-predator-should-never-become-president/

"I'M NOT A SOCIALIST" – Joe Biden
"Make no mistake: Joe Biden is not a moderate. He is the most left-wing nominee his party has ever put forward. He has enlisted Bernie Sanders and Alexandria Ocasio-Cortez to craft his administration's policy positions. Here is a quick guide to some of Joe Biden's extreme positions." – The Hill

BIDEN SUPPORTS FREE HEALTHCARE FOR ILLEGAL IMMIGRANTS
"Biden says he believes there is 'an obligation' to provide health insurance for undocumented immigrants. Such coverage wasn't provided under ObamaCare." – The Hill

Biden Said The United States Is Obligated To Give Health Care To Everyone, "Regardless Of Whether They Are Documented Or Undocumented." – Free Beacon

"Every Democratic Presidential Candidate Onstage At The Second Night Of The Debate Raised Their Hand When Asked If They Would Extend Health Care Coverage To Undocumented Immigrants." – Buzzfeed

BIDEN SUPPORTS TAXPAYER FUNDING OF ABORTION
"Former Vice President Joe Biden said Thursday he is against the Hyde Amendment, which bans federal funding for abortions in most cases, reversing course from his earlier position after criticism from his 2020 Democratic rivals." – CBS News

BIDEN SUPPORTS CITIZENSHIP FOR 11 MILLION ILLEGAL IMMIGRANTS

"Joe Biden will work with Congress to pass legislation that: **Creates a roadmap to citizenship for the nearly 11 million people who have been living in and strengthening our country for years**. *Biden will aggressively advocate for legislation that creates a clear roadmap to legal status and citizenship for unauthorized immigrants who register, are up-to-date on their taxes, and have passed a background check."* – Joe Biden Campaign Website

Simply put: This is de facto amnesty. Since illegal immigrants largely do not pay income taxes; then it can be assumed that "up-to-date on their taxes" in Biden's plan means every illegal immigrant who has not paid US income taxes would be considered "up-to-date- on their taxes". Additionally, Biden has yet to explain how expansive a background check would be. Additionally, this implies that Biden does not believe that living in the United States illegally is a crime.

BIDEN PLEDGES TO STOP IMMIGRATION ENFORCEMENT

"President Biden will end workplace raids to ensure that threats based on workers' status do not interfere with their ability to organize and improve their wages and working conditions. He will also protect sensitive locations from immigration enforcement actions. No one should be afraid to seek medical attention, go to school, their job, or their place of worship for fear of an immigration enforcement action." – Joe Biden Campaign Website

"READ JOE BIDEN'S LIPS: NEW TAXES" – WALL STREET JOURNAL EDITORIAL BOARD"

"Revenue estimates for Mr. Biden's tax agenda vary, from $4 trillion over a decade to $3.2 trillion, after accounting for how it would shrink the economy. But analysts confirm the phoniness of Mr. Biden's pledge. ***Over the long run, the Tax Foundation said in April, his main tax proposals would lower after-tax incomes for every quintile, including 1.4% for the middle class.***

An American Enterprise Institute study from June assumed that a fifth of the higher corporate tax would fall on workers "in the form of lower compensation." If so, taxpayers in the 80% to 90% decile, earning around $170,000 to $248,000, would carry an additional $725 tax burden in 2021, on average. For those in the 90% to 95% range, earning less than $353,000, the figure would be $1,368. "Overall," the report says, "24.7 percent of new tax revenue in 2021 would come from the bottom 99 percent of taxpayers."

That's before Mr. Biden has to figure out how to pay for the full spending agenda he is laying out for the left. He claims his tax proposals will soak only the affluent, but they won't raise nearly enough money to

finance all of his plans. In the end everyone will pay." – Wall Street Journal

JOE BIDEN'S CLIMATE AGENDA WILL HALT AMERICAN ENERGY PRODUCTION AND END THOUSANDS OF JOBS

"When it comes to energy policy, presumptive Democratic nominee Joe Biden has a lot of cleaning up to do as he now begins to move into general election mode in his campaign. The clean-up job will not be easy.

During the primary season, as he worked to secure the votes of his Party's left-leaning voter base, Mr. Biden has promised at various times to enforce a policy of "no new fracking" in his administration; to end the use of oil and natural gas in the United States; and to end new drilling on federal lands in the U.S. While promises like those and others played well to the voters in Party primaries around the country, they have the potential to come back to haunt Biden during the general election in key swing states like Michigan, Pennsylvania, Ohio and New Mexico, where the industry supports hundreds of thousands of jobs and the state governments rely heavily on income from oil and gas taxes.

Make no mistake: These impacts are huge. A recent study released by the Marcellus Shale Coalition calculated that a ban on fracking in that state would cost 609,000 jobs and eliminate $261 billion in economic impact and cost the state government $23.4 billion in annual income." – Forbes

BIDEN SAYS HIS #1 LEGISLATIVE PRIORITY IS PASSING A "GENDER RIGHTS" LAW WHICH WOULD CHANGE SOCIETY

Joe Biden stated that his number one legislative priority as president would be to pass a piece legislation called the "Equality Act". While the name sounds positive, the truth is this is a very extreme bill which has a variety of mandates such as:

- *Giving biological males the right to compete in female sports nationwide.*
- *Giving biological males the right to use any female facilities such as bathrooms and locker rooms nationwide.*
- *Require doctors to perform life-altering gender-transition procedures on children under the age of 18, even without the consent of their parents.*
- *Mandating gender-transition and choice as a right. This could potentially cause parents to lose custody of children who believe they are of a different gender than their biological one.*
- *Forcing any person, business, or religious institution to violate their religious beliefs to comply with the Act.*

Sources:
A Pediatrician Explains How 'Dangerous' Equality Act Would Force Doctors to 'Do Harm'
HERITAGE EXPLAINS The Equality Act
The 'Equality Act' is a threat to women's sports
Biden declares LGBTQ rights his No. 1 legislative priority
Equality Act

"I'M A PATRIOT" – Joe Biden
VP BIDEN ADVISED AGAINST THE BIN LADEN RAID

"Vice President Joe Biden confessed this weekend that he advised President Obama not to launch the mission that ultimately killed Osama bin Laden last spring. During remarks at a Democratic congressional retreat this weekend, Biden explained that when it came time to make the final decision, he had some lingering uncertainties about whether the 9/11 mastermind was in the suspected compound in Pakistan." – ABC News

BIDEN'S FLAWED CALCULATIONS CLEARED THE WAY FOR PRO-IRANIAN INFLUENCE IN IRAQ

Former vice president Joe Biden reportedly played a decisive role in enabling recently assassinated Iranian terror leader Qassem Soleimani to push the United States out of Iraq and deliver the country into the hands of Iran.

In 2010, as Iraq faced pivotal elections that decided the country's direction, Soleimani went to great lengths to ensure Iranian-backed politicians won control of the government, according to a comprehensive 2013 New Yorker profile of the terror leader by Dexter Filkins.

During that time, Filkins reported, then-vice president Biden called pro-America Iraqi politician Ayad Allawi to demand he stop trying to form a government. This crucial call paved the way for Soleimani to orchestrate an Iranian takeover of the Iraqi political system, according to interviews Filkins conducted with numerous sources.

JOE BIDEN LIED ABOUT BENGHAZI (ONE MONTH BEFORE 2012 ELECTION)

"Vice President Joe Biden claimed that the administration wasn't aware of requests for more security in Libya before the Sept. 11 attacks on the U.S. mission in Benghazi during Thursday night's debate, contradicting two State Department officials and the former head of diplomatic security in Libya.

"We weren't told they wanted more security. We did not know they wanted more security there," Biden said. In fact, two security officials who worked for the State Department in Libya at the time testified

Thursday that they repeatedly requested more security and two State Department officials admitted they had denied those requests." – Foreign Policy

"I NEVER SAID THAT" – Joe Biden's response to Kamala Harris's anti-busing accusation, 2019 Debates

IN ORDER TO PRESERVE HIS POLITICAL CAREER, JOE BIDEN ACTIVELY FOUGHT SCHOOL INTEGRATION THROUGH BUSING

In the early-70's, Joe Biden was a freshly elected Senator from Delaware. Wilmington (Delaware's largest city) was facing action from federal court (Evans v. Buchanan 1974) as a result of it's largely segregated schools. One of the remedies cities used was desegregation busing. Senator Biden opposed busing and integration in an effort to preserve his political career.

"He emerged as the Democratic Party's leading anti-busing crusader — a position that put him in league with Southern segregationists, at odds with liberal Republicans and helped change the dynamic of the Senate, turning even some leaders in his own party against busing as a desegregation tool. "No issue has consumed more of my time and energies," Mr. Biden declared with a flourish as he opened a Senate hearing in 1981, adding, "We want to stop court-ordered busing." – New York Times

"In the summer of 1974, the freshman Senator Joe Biden found himself under siege from white suburbanites at a meeting just south of Wilmington, Del. The possibility that their children would be bused into "black schools" in the city and that black children would be bused to their schools had sent a wave of consternation through the white community. Civil rights activists had recently won a lawsuit in which a federal District Court recognized that state-sponsored discriminatory education and housing policies had led to segregated metropolitan-area schools. The court was then poised to demand a two-way busing program that would transfer students between the city and suburban districts to advance racial balance. For two hours, Biden paced the auditorium stage and absorbed the ire of the 250-member audience. Unable to offer them any assurance on the court ruling, he made a promise to oppose busing when he returned to Washington for the next legislative session. And he did: Biden spent the next four years pushing legislation to thwart the implementation of busing schemes like the one demanded by the courts in Wilmington around the country." – Politico

"I'M NOT A RACIST" – Joe Biden

JOE BIDEN HAS A HISTORY OF CONTROVERSIAL RACIAL COMMENTS

"Amid the fallout from comments by former vice president and presumptive Democratic presidential nominee, Joe Biden, about a lack of diversity of thought and heritage within the African American community, some worry that a pattern of blunders could impact support within the Black community. Biden drew criticism on Thursday when he compared the diversity of African American and Latino communities at a pretaped virtual talk with the National Association of Black Journalists and the National Association of Hispanic Journalists. "What you all know, but most people don't know. Unlike the African American community, with notable exceptions, the Latino community is an incredibly diverse community with incredibly different attitudes about different things," Biden said." – MSN

Joe Biden made waves Friday (May 22, 2020) when he said that African-Americans unsure of whether they should vote for President Trump or him "ain't black," but it was hardly the first time the 77-year-old has come under criticism for a racially charged remark. Here's a look at past controversies over Biden's comments:

May 2020: "You ain't black."

In an interview with "The Breakfast Club," the presumptive Democratic nominee told host Charlamagne tha God, "I tell you if you have a problem figuring out whether you're for me or Trump, then you ain't black," before defending his record with the black community.

August 2019: "Poor kids" just as bright as "white kids."

At a campaign event in Iowa, Biden told supporters "poor kids are just as bright and talented as white kids." He quickly corrected himself after some applause by adding: "Wealthy kids, black kids, Asian kids."

August 2012: "Put y'all back in chains."

Then-Vice President Biden told a Virginia audience that then-Republican presidential candidate Mitt Romney's financial regulation lifts would "put y'all back in chains." "He said in the first 100 days, he's going to let the big banks once again write their own rules," Biden said. "Unchain Wall Street! They're gonna put y'all back in chains."

February 2007: Obama is "the first mainstream African-American who is articulate and bright and clean."

Biden, while running for the 2008 presidency, issued what he thought was praise of then-Senator Barack Obama, saying he was "the first mainstream African-American who is articulate and bright and clean." – Fox News

Among stories readers widely shared was a July 15, 2019, Business Insider story that reported, "Former Vice President Joe Biden is facing increased scrutiny over his record on busing and racial issues, and this

week old comments resurfaced in which he said, in 1977, that busing for the purpose of desegregation would cause his children to 'grow up in a racial jungle.

The quote is accurate as reported and reads in full: "Unless we do something about this, my children are going to grow up in a jungle, the jungle being a racial jungle with tensions having built so high that it is going to explode at some point. We have got to make some move on this." – Snopes

"JOE'S A DECENT MAN" – multiple testimonials during the D.N.C.

JOE BIDEN IS KNOWN TO LASH OUT AT INDIVIDUALS WHO QUESTION HIM

*Biden told a Detroit autoworker they are "full of sh**!" and told him to not be "such a horses a**!"* – Fox News

Biden lashed out at a New Hampshire voter calling her a "lying dog-faced pony soldier." – The Gateway Pundit

Biden tore into an Iowa democrat voter over his question about Hunter Biden's shady Ukraine work. "Former Vice President Joe Biden on Thursday (12/5/19) got in a tense back-and-forth with an audience member during an Iowa campaign stop after the man made debunked claims that the former vice president sent his son Hunter Biden to work for an energy company in Ukraine. "You're a damn liar, man. That's not true," Biden shot back at the man, who said the claims, which have been circulated by some on the right, were backed up by reporting on television. After some cross-talk, Biden told the man, "By the way ... I'm not sedentary," before going on to challenge him to a push-up contest and other physical tests." – The Hill

Sources:

The Joe Biden Busing Problem

Joe Biden tells a man he's full of s***.

Joe Biden tears into a voter who asks him a question.

"ONLY THOSE WITH INCOMES ABOVE $400,000 WILL BE TAXED"
– Joe Biden, August 23rd, 2020 ABC interview

JOE BIDEN TO RICH DONORS: "NOTHING WOULD FUNDAMENTALLY CHANGE" IF HE'S ELECTED

Along with praise for the "civility" of racists, Biden assures donors "no one's standard of living will change"

Igor Derysh. Salon.

More here: https://www.salon.com/2019/06/19/joe-biden-to-rich-donors-nothing-would-fundmentally-change-if-hcs-elected/

June 19th 2019, 9:00pm (UTC)

Former Vice President Joe Biden assured rich donors at a ritzy New York fundraiser that "nothing would fundamentally change" if he is elected. Biden told donors at an event at the Carlyle Hotel in Manhattan on Tuesday evening that he would not "demonize" the rich and promised that "no one's standard of living will change, nothing would fundamentally change," Bloomberg News reported.

Biden's assurance to donors in New York came shortly after his appearance at the Poor People's Campaign Presidential Forum in Washington on Monday. Biden said that poverty was "the one thing that can bring this country down" and listed several new programs to help the poor that he would fund if elected. "We have all the money we need to do it," he said. But speaking to wealthy donors in New York, Biden appeared to suggest that his plan would not involve big tax hikes on the rich. "I mean, we may not want to demonize anybody who has made money," he said. "The truth of the matter is, you all, you all know, you all know in your gut what has to be done. We can disagree in the margins but the truth of the matter is it's all within our wheelhouse and nobody has to be punished. No one's standard of living will change, nothing would fundamentally change."

Biden went on to say that the rich should not be blamed for income inequality, pleading to the donors, "I need you very badly." "I hope if I win this nomination, I won't let you down. I promise you," he added. Biden also complained that some Democrats criticized his eagerness to work with Republicans after they spent years blocking President Obama's agenda and moving further right.

Biden pointed out that his ability to work with segregationists like former Mississippi Sen. James O. Eastland and Georgia Sen. Herman Talmadge showed that he could "bring people together," The Washington Post reported. "I was in a caucus with James O. Eastland," Biden said. "He never called me 'boy,' he always called me 'son.'" He also cited Talmadge, calling him "one of the meanest guys I ever knew."

"Well, guess what?" Biden said. "At least there was some civility. We got things done. We didn't agree on much of anything. We got things done. We got it finished. But today, you look at the other side and you're the enemy. Not the opposition — the enemy. We don't talk to each other anymore."

"I know the new 'New Left' tells me that I'm — this is old-fashioned," he added. "Well guess what? If we can't reach a consensus in our system, what happens? It encourages and demands the abuse of power by a president. That's what it does. You have to be able to reach consensus under our system — our constitutional system of separation of powers."

Sen. Cory Booker of New Jersey, one of Biden's Democratic opponents, issued a statement condemning the former vice president's comment. "You don't joke about calling black men 'boys,'" said Booker, who is black. "Men like James O. Eastland used words like that, and the racist policies that accompanied them, to perpetuate white supremacy and strip black Americans of our very humanity. Vice President Biden's relationship with proud segregationists are not the model for how we make America a safer and more inclusive place for black people, and for everyone," Booker added. "And frankly, I'm disappointed that he hasn't issued an immediate apology for the pain his words are dredging up for many Americans. He should."

*New York Mayor Bill de Blasio, who is also running for president, slammed Biden's comments in a tweet featuring a photo of his mixed-race family. "It's 2019 & [Biden] is longing for the good old days of 'civility' typified by James Eastland. Eastland thought my multiracial family should be illegal & that whites were entitled to 'the pursuit of dead n*ggers,'" De Blasio wrote. "It's past time for apologies or evolution from [Biden]. He repeatedly demonstrates that he is out of step with the values of the modern Democratic Party."*

It's become very clear that Biden appeared to be doing nothing up front because he's been working diligently behind the scenes lining his family's pockets and stabbing taxpayers in their collective backs while he does it. After reading the grand socialist schemes in his "vision" for his presidency at joebiden.com and listening to his rhetoric it's easy to see that he's gonna do his damnedest to screw Americans further by unionizing the entire country, which will allow them to feast on every working Americans' paycheck unfettered, much like they're doing now but on a grander scale, because they'll have the backing of a president that was taught covert socialism by the best, Barack Obama.

TIGERS DON'T CHANGE THEIR STRIPES

A point to ponder: Biden's been in politics for forty-seven years. In that time he's been on the wrong side of every issue and presided over the offshore concealment of corporations' money, the shipping of jobs to Mexico and China, the globalization of manufacturing businesses that were once American, and the destruction of the middle class by things like Obamacare, onerous regulations, and lining union executives' pockets causing the slowest economic recovery on record. He cheered for all of it, still does in fact. You'd have to be an extra-special kind of stupid to believe he's gonna reverse course and undo the damage he's done to this country, especially the damage his socialist mentor, Obama, did and he champions to this day.

WHO'S WHO?

In one corner there's the delusionary corporatist Trump/Pence combo that's built what progress it's made on the lie of doing it for the people while the corporations were the ones that prospered. In the other there's the cancel culture socialists, Biden/Harris, who've done nothing but pat themselves on the back for making a career out of making excuses for doing nothing and blaming others for the problems their ideologies create. Grab your asses and bend right over! You're screwed again no matter who you elect and they're both too cheap to pay for Vaseline.

SCREWED AGAIN

For several decades I've maintained that the best way to tell the elite we're done playing their game(s) is refusing to vote for the idiots they select as "candidates." However, you've been so thoroughly indoctrinated in their rigged system you believe their "if you don't vote you can't complain" propaganda and that the next election will be the one that breaks the 244-year cycle of getting screwed by the wealthy. Insanity is doing the same thing over and over while expecting a different outcome. That applies to one person, one nation, and/or one world.

"I HAVE SOLVED THIS DILEMMA IN A VERY DIRECT WAY: I DON'T VOTE. ON ELECTION DAY I STAY HOME. I FIRMLY BELIEVE THAT IF YOU VOTE, YOU HAVE NO RIGHT TO COMPLAIN. NOW SOME PEOPLE LIKE TO TWIST THAT AROUND. THEY SAY, "IF YOU DON'T VOTE YOU HAVE NO RIGHT TO COMPLAIN," BUT WHERE'S THE LOGIC IN THAT? IF YOU VOTE, AND YOU ELECT DISHONEST, INCOMPETENT POLITICIANS, AND THE THEY GET INTO OFFICE AND SCREW EVERYTHING UP, YOU ARE RESPONSIBLE FOR WHAT THEY HAVE DONE. YOU VOTED THEM IN. YOU CAUSED THE PROBLEM." – George Carlin

The very bottom line is that no matter what idiot occupies the White House nothing of much consequence will change because the elite that control every aspect of this world won't allow it. They have their own agenda and it doesn't involve caring about what people need or want, it's strictly about filling their coffers any and every way possible. Why would they care about something they consider useless breeders/eaters, cannon fodder, and commodities? That sentiment will only deepen as AI takes over the jobs people now do, forcing them to institute a U.B.I., as evidenced by their multiple proclamations and publications that call for radical depopulation.

END GLOBALIZATION

There's no greater argument for ending the insanity of globalization than the shortages of PPE, test kits, and the necessities required to mitigate the Covid-19 outbreak due to the world's supply of necessary items being manufactured in one country; that country being on lockdown because the virus it created is rampant there; a country that's actually an enemy with a global dominance agenda, willing to use any means at its disposal to attain that goal, including the extermination of as much of the global population as possible in order to reduce its ability to resist its single party Maoist regime's takeover agenda.

Another argument against it is the massive and totally unnecessary pollution created by shipping raw materials around the globe to manufacturing sites and shipping the finished products around the globe once again to consumers. This form of unprecedented greed driven insanity based solely on the bottomlines of the elite's companies with no basis in common sense is responsible for a large part of the gaseous and particulate content polluting the atmosphere.

Those profiting mightily from globalization will cry "isolationism" over this sentiment but that's only because we're either a commodity or cannon fodder to them and ending globalism would destroy their ability to profit from the animosity and competition it generates between countries and the wars that creates as nations compete both financially and physically for a piece of the global market.

The global shutdown due to the Covid-19 outbreak proves beyond a shadow of a doubt that ending globalism will drastically reduce the pollution created by its accompanying industrialization and commerce very quickly. Within the first week manufacturing and shipping stopped there was a noticeable decrease in the carbonization of the atmosphere that increased throughout the shutdown. People in China remarked that it was the first time in decades they had seen the sunrise and sunset because the skies were clear.

CONTAGION 2020

The following articles are presented in toto due to the amount of information they contain. I suggest you use the links provided here to view the articles online because there are quite a few links to connected articles embedded in each one.

COVID-19 MAY BE MAN-MADE, CLAIMS TAIWAN SCHOLAR

A professor at the National Taiwan University claims the highly infectious virus could be 'synthetic'.

By Frank Chen. Asia Times.
More here: https://asiatimes.com/2020/02/covid-19-may-be-man-made-claims-taiwan-scholar/
February 25th 2020

As scientists, doctors, academics and conspiracy theorists toss around ideas and speculate on where the highly infectious virus originated, **a professor in etiology at the National Taiwan University has claimed that the highly infectious virus could be "synthetic" in nature – in other words, man-made***.*

Questions about the exact origin of the novel coronavirus have grown as it spread across China and then beyond. Hubei, the central Chinese province where it first erupted, reported 499 new cases on Tuesday, while South Korea, Japan, Singapore and Italy have become the new frontiers in the battle to contain the contagion.

Speculation has grown about how the Covid-19 virus came into being. The official conclusion by Chinese authorities is that a dingy wet market in Wuhan – Hubei's capital – was the source of the respiratory pathogen as animal-human transmission could have occurred there. There has been much speculation about a virology institute in the city, affiliated with the Chinese Academy of Sciences, with rumors about a leakage due to slack management triggering a public health crisis worse than the SARS incident of 2003.

Some of the more nonsensical talk includes a conspiracy theory that the United States "made" the virus to mass-infect Chinese people and stop the rise of its arch-rival. *Now a professor in etiology at the National Taiwan University has claimed the highly infectious virus could be "synthetic" in nature, or man-made.* ***"Researchers likely synthesized the Covid-19, although more studies are needed to be certain,"*** *NTU professor Fang Chi-tai told a forum on disease control and prevention in Taipei held by the Taiwan Public Health Association earlier this month. During his presentation, Fang outlined several hypotheses raised by Taiwanese and overseas researchers, including the probability that the virus was "man-made" and was leaked from the Wuhan Institute of Virology due to gross mismanagement.*

Fang said the Wuhan facility's biosafety level-4 laboratory was used to store, handle and research samples of SARS, Ebola and other deadly infectious viruses. ***"Given China's poor track record of lab safety management, including a leakage of the SARS virus at a state lab in 2004, it is possible that a virus escaped from the Wuhan facility and*** *resulted in the epidemic," Fang was quoted by Taiwan's Central News Agency and the Taipei Times as saying.*

He added that analyses of **the Covid-19 virus have shown that it had a 96% genetic similarity with an RaTG13 bat virus also stored at the institute, and that the Covid-19 could be "manufactured" by modifying the RaTG13 virus.** <u>**Fang also revealed that French researchers had discovered four more amino acids in the gene sequence of Covid-19 than other known coronaviruses, which could be added artificially to make the viral transmission easier.**</u> <u>**Fang's theory is that natural mutations of viruses will only result in small, singular changes, and it is suspicious to see a naturally mutated virus suddenly take on four amino acids**</u>. *Determining the source of the virus would have important implications for epidemiology, he added, saying that* **if the virus was indeed synthetic, then it could be easier for it to be eradicated.**

Meanwhile, **Taiwan's top research institute Academia Sinica said its researchers had already developed an antibody testing method for Covid-19 infection and made encouraging progress in synthesizing remdesivir, a medicine that many believe could cure the infection.**

Taiwan's Center for Disease Control on Tuesday sent serum samples from three people who had contact with Taiwan's first Covid-19 fatality to the Academia Sinica, as part of a joint effort to determine the source of that infection and if the three had developed antibodies. The initial tests showed that only one sample had antibodies for Covid-19 and SARS. The sample was obtained from a Taiwanese businessperson who was not listed as a confirmed case, as researchers believed his immune system had beaten the virus. Yet the institute said it was still a mystery whether a person who had recovered from a novel coronavirus infection could contract it again.

Another team at Taiwan's Institute of Chemistry has also succeeded in synthesizing 100mg of remdesivir. The synthesized drug cannot be used without the consent of a US pharmaceutical firm that manufactures remdesivir. *It was reported that Taiwan was negotiating a technology transfer deal to start mass production of the antiviral drug.*

Remdesivir is a novel drug developed by the California-based Gilead Sciences as a treatment for Ebola virus and Murburg virus infections, and it has subsequently been found to show antiviral activity against other viruses.

Based on its success against other coronavirus infections, Gilead provided remdesivir to physicians that treated an American patient infected with Covid-19 and was offering the compound to China for a pair of trials in infected individuals with and without severe symptoms.

The mystery of how and where the virus started may take longer to discover than the cure.

CORONAVIRUS 'LAB LEAKAGE' RUMORS SPREADING

Outbreak 'could have started' in Wuhan facility, as first patient never went to wet market identified as source.

By Frank Chen. Asia Times.

More here: https://asiatimes.com/2020/02/coronavirus-lab-leakage-rumors-spreading/

February 17th 2020

A Wuhan lab affiliated with the Chinese Academy of Sciences has sought to dispel rumors that it "made and leaked" the highly infectious pneumonic virus that led to the still-raging global outbreak. **While Chinese President Xi Jinping was briefed about the public health threat by the Chinese Center for Disease Control and Prevention (CCDC) in early January, the government decided against sounding the alarm because it did not want to "mar the festive vibe" during the Lunar New Year celebrations.**

The Wuhan Institute of Virology, located in the provincial capital of Hubei, which is the ground zero of the contagion, has been thrust into the media spotlight by the allegation last week that it leaked "bio-hazardous agents."

Posts circulating on WeChat and Weibo claim that a researcher at the institute was the first to be infected by the novel coronavirus, now called Covid-19 by the World Health Organization. The female virologist and a graduate from the institute, referred to as "patient zero," had never visited the city's shambolic wet market – also known as the "zoo" *– where a range of wild animals were sold. The market has been identified by the authorities as the most probable source of the deadly pathogen. In a statement released on Sunday, the lab stressed that the researcher had left the city in 2015 and was in good health, refusing to release more information about her for privacy reasons.*

The institute is said to be the nation's only Biological Security Level 4-certified lab, the highest level in the hierarchy of biosafety and biocontainment procedures codified by the US Center for Disease Control and Prevention. The Wuhan lab has the equipment and staff to handle the most infectious viruses, including Ebola.

Shi Zhengli, the institute's lead researcher on bat-related viruses, said on her social media account that she "guaranteed with her own life" that the outbreak had nothing to do with the lab but was a "nemesis for the barbaric habits and lifestyle of some people – like eating wild game including bats." Shi's team said at the end of January, when the acute respiratory disease started to strike down more people in Wuhan and the rest of Hubei, that bats could have been the initial host of the coronavirus and SARS virus. Shi also heads an expert panel advising the Hubei provincial government in the battle against the epidemic.

Richard Ebright, a biology professor at Rutgers University in New Jersey, told the BBC that genomic sequencing of the coronavirus showed no proof that it had been artificially modified, yet he could not rule out the possibility that the unfolding pandemic could be the result of a "lab incident." *Ebright said the coronavirus was a cousin of one found in bats captured by the institute in caves in the southwestern province of Yunnan in 2003, and that samples had been kept in the Wuhan lab since 2013.*

Also, a paper that appeared in the prestigious medical journal The Lancet at the end of last month has lent credibility to speculation about the origins of the virus. ***The paper quoted seven doctors at Wuhan's Jinyintan Hospital as saying that the first patient admitted on December 1 had "never been to the wet market," nor had there been any epidemiological link between the first patient and subsequent infection cases, based on the data from the first 41 patients treated there.*** *Furthermore, a note from the Chinese Ministry of Science and Technology is seen as a tacit admission that some kind of incident may have occurred at the Wuhan lab.*

On Saturday, the ministry issued a directive mandating more stringent handling of viruses and bioagents by all labs and research institutes. The document alluded to the slack oversight and management rampant at some facilities, and stressed that protection and decontamination must be beefed up now that more labs across the nation are intensifying their efforts to develop medicines to treat it and a vaccine to prevent it.

Meanwhile, Hong Kong's Ming Pao daily reported on Monday that the CCDC had sounded the alarm in a report on the emerging SARS-like outbreak submitted to the top leadership in early January. However, ***curbing the spread was not at the top of the agenda when Xi and other members of the party's upper echelon sat down for a Politburo meeting on January 7. Citing its source, the broadsheet said top leaders were opposed to any contingency measures "that may mar the festive vibe and make the public panic."***

In a move seen as a bid to highlight Xi's early involvement in combating the outbreak, state media revealed on Sunday that the president "gave specific instructions" to contain the spread in the January 7 meeting, amid people's simmering exasperation with the state and local cadres' tardy response to the public health crisis that has made more than 70,000 sick across the country as of Monday afternoon. And even though the CCDC alerted Xi early on, its chief, Gao Fu, is still under fire for his public assurances last month that people were not likely to become infected as a result of normal human contact. Calls are being made for Gao, a veterinarian by training, to step down.

ANGER AS WUHAN VIRUS KILLS WHISTLEBLOWER
Li Wenliang, a hospital ophthalmologist, sounded the alarm when cadres tried to cover up the deadly outbreak

By Frank Chen. Asia Times.
More here: https://asiatimes.com/2020/02/anger-as-wuhan-virus-kills-whistleblower/?_=4977507
February 7th 2020

The army of censors employed by the Communist Party's propaganda apparatus has apparently failed to muzzle the massive outpouring of grief and anger since midnight, when news about the death of Li Wenliang found its way onto social media platforms. **Li, 34, an ophthalmologist who singlehandedly blew the lid off the growing novel coronavirus epidemic in Wuhan in central China's Hubei province, was once detained and reprimanded by the city's police for "fear-mongering." This was after he revealed in a WeChat group on December 30 that seven patients showing SARS-like symptoms had been admitted to Wuhan Central Hospital, where he worked.**

Li, together with seven other "agitators," was summoned by the police on January 3 and forced to make a confession, after Wuhan's government and the National Health Commission sought to hush up the situation on the ground, in orchestrated moves with the media including the state broadcaster China Central Television, to name and shame Li and other "rumormongers."

Yet before long, **what was rejected by party cadres and state media as "pure fabrication" soon turned into fact within the span of a few weeks, when the deadly pneumonic virus, once latent in Wuhan, began to infect people in other provinces, leading to an about-face by cadres and state media, who issued belated alerts as they found it was no longer possible to hide the outbreak.**

Li later told reporters that initially he was perturbed by his warning being relayed by netizens as he only wanted to remind his friends to be vigilant, but soon realized that the public's right to know during a crisis must be respected. "A healthy society must not have only one voice," Li was quoted as saying.

Li, known across the nation as the first whistleblower to reveal the official coverup, was infected with the virus he warned of at the end of January, apparently from an eye patient he treated. His case was confirmed on February 1 at his hospital and he remained in the intensive care unit as his condition steadily worsened.

On Thursday evening, leading publications in China reported that Li had died, and the China News Weekly and Economic Observer quoted his colleagues as saying that in his last few hours Li drifted in and out of coma, his life sustained with the help of extra-corporeal membrane oxygenation, hinting that his resuscitation could have been delayed. Wuhan's government said on Friday morning that it was "saddened" by Li's death. Li is survived by his wife, who is pregnant with a second child and is also said to be battling for her own life after being infected with the same virus.

*Grief and anger started to permeate WeChat and Weibo from late Thursday. Netizens mourned Li's death and praised him for having the courage to tell the truth. Censors, overwhelmed by the sudden burst of strong emotions, fumbled to respond, as initially they were not given clear instructions on how to respond to the avalanche of posts honoring Li. **The strong expression of sympathy and frustration has morphed into a rare display of the pervasive, seething wrath of the people, as they realize that, yet again, central and local officials often try to downplay or conceal crises and will do anything to restore a semblance of normality**. They are angry that a brave young doctor who dared to reveal the truth has died, some suspect because of belated treatment by the authorities, and that the cadres who lied are getting off with a rap on the knuckles.*

*****There is also growing exasperation over how President Xi Jinping has handled the crisis. He has made only a few public appearances in the past two weeks – meeting with World Health Organization Director-General Tedros Adhanom on January 28**, receiving Cambodian Prime Minister Hun Sen on February 5, and presiding over a Politburo meeting on Wednesday. **The top leader has not left Zhongnanhai since the epidemic spread across the nation and appears to be more willing to talk to foreign dignitaries about fighting the disease than to his own people**. Meanwhile, the party's central discipline and inspection committee said on Friday afternoon that it would dispatch a task force to Wuhan to probe "issues related to Dr Li."*

CORONAVIRUS OUTBREAK A RESULT OF CHINESE BIOLOGICAL ESPIONAGE?

Did Chinese biological warfare program agents smuggle the virus into the country?

Web Desk. The Week.

More here: https://www.theweek.in/news/world/2020/01/28/coronavirus-outbreak-a-result-of-chinese-biological-espionage.html

January 28th 2020 16:25 IST

China's coronavirus outbreak dubbed as Wuhan virus has already seen the death toll cross 100 with thousands said to have been infected in the region. While measures are being taken to contain the virus and find a cure, **there is growing reports that the virus may not have originated from the seafood market as claimed by China, but from a laboratory not far from the reported ground zero***.*

The Wuhan Institute of Virology National Biosafety Laboratory which is a Level 4 certified lab that is capable of conducting research activities involving Ebola, Nipah and other deadly viruses. The Wuhan National Biosafety Laboratory is located only 32 kms away from the Hunan Seafood market which has been named as the epicentre of the virus outbreak. The Chinese government has remained silent even as the number of reports questioning the virus' origin has increased.

According to investigations done by online portal GreatGameIndia the origin of the virus can be traced to Canada and two Chinese biological warfare program agents who smuggled it into China*. The report goes as follows: On June 13, 2012 a 60-year-old Saudi man was admitted to a private hospital in Jeddah, Saudi Arabia, with a 7-day history of fever, cough, expectoration, and shortness of breath. He had no history of cardiopulmonary or renal disease, was receiving no long-term medications, and did not smoke. Egyptian virologist Dr. Ali Mohamed Zaki isolated and identified a previously unknown coronavirus from his lungs. After routine diagnostics failed to identify the causative agent, Zaki contacted Ron Fouchier, a leading virologist at the Erasmus Medical Center (EMC) in Rotterdam, the Netherlands, for advice.*

Fouchier sequenced the virus from a sample sent by Zaki. Fouchier used a broad-spectrum 'pan-coronavirus'' real-time polymerase chain reaction (RT-PCR) method to test for distinguishing features of a number of known coronaviruses known to infect humans. **This coronavirus sample was acquired by Scientific Director Dr. Frank Plummer of Canada's National Microbiology Laboratory (NML) in Winnipeg** *directly from Fouchier, who received it from Zaki. This virus was reportedly stolen from the Canadian lab by Chinese agents.*

In March 2019, in mysterious event a shipment of exceptionally virulent viruses from Canada's NML ended up in China. The event caused a major scandal with Bio-warfare experts questioning why Canada was sending lethal viruses to China. *Scientists from NML said the highly lethal viruses were a potential bio-weapon. Following investigation, the incident was traced to Chinese agents working at NML. Four months later in July 2019, a group of Chinese virologists were forcibly dispatched from the Canadian National Microbiology Laboratory (NML).* The NML is Canada's only level-4 facility and one of only a few in North America equipped to handle the world's deadliest diseases, including Ebola, SARS, Coronavirus, etc.

While there is no proof that the virus outbreak was intentional, **James Giordano, a neurology professor at Georgetown University and senior fellow in Biowarfare at the US Special Operations Command said that China's growing investment in bio-science, looser ethics around gene-editing raise the spectre of such pathogens being weaponised. It could also mean that such an offensive agent could benefit China which might have the only treatment or vaccine.**

While the number of conspiracy theories have been on the rise, silence from the Chinese government regarding these theories is adding fuel to speculations. With many countries issuing travel adversaries to its citizens against traveling to China, the coronavirus outbreak has certainly hit the Chinese tourism industry during their biggest travel period.

QUESTIONS SURROUND CANADIAN SHIPMENT OF DEADLY VIRUSES TO CHINA

The same Winnipeg lab that sent Ebola and Henipah viruses to Beijing recently removed a number of researchers for an "administrative issue."

Nicoletta Lanese. The Scientist Magazine.
More here: https://www.the-scientist.com/news-opinion/questions-surround-canadian-shipment-of-deadly-viruses-to-china-66254
Aug 9th 2019

Canada's National Microbiology Laboratory shipped Ebola and Henipah viruses to Beijing on March 31, raising suspicions from experts in biochemical warfare, who say they think China may use the pathogens to develop offensive biological agents.

The Public Health Agency of Canada (PHAC) and the Royal Canadian Mounted Police (RCMP) report that the incident has not introduced any known risk to public health, according to the Winnipeg Free Press.

The same lab is the focus of an ongoing investigation by the RCMP. The inquiry began following the recent dismissal of the head of the National Microbiology Laboratory's (NML) Vaccine Development and Antiviral Therapies section in the Special Pathogens Program, virologist Xiangguo Qiu. Qiu, her colleague and husband Keding Cheng, and a number of her international students lost security clearance to their lab on July 5.

In 2018, Governor General Julie Payette presented Qiu with an innovation award for her helping to lead the development of the Ebola vaccine Zmapp, according to the Winnipeg Free Press. There are no reports as to whether she was involved in the March shipment.

Ebola and Henipah viruses—classified as Category A and C bioterrorism agents by the US Centers for Disease Control and Prevention, respectively—pose a threat to national security because of their potential to be easily disseminated, cause high morbidity and mortality rates, and deliver lasting blows to public health. They are also categorized as Risk Group 4 pathogens, meaning they can only be handled in a lab with the highest level of biosafety control, according to CBC News.

"All transfers of Risk Group 4 samples follow strict transportation requirements and are authorized by senior officials at the lab and the NML tracks and keeps electronic records of all shipments of samples in accordance with the HPTA," PHAC spokesman Eric Morrissette writes in a statement, as reported by CBC News. "On the specific shipments to China earlier this year, we can confirm that we have all records pertaining to the shipment, and that all protocols were followed as directed by the above Acts and Standards."

Although health officials insist all protocols were met, anonymous sources report that the shipment lacked an agreement spelling out intellectual property rights, known as a "material transfer agreement," according to the Winnipeg Free Press. The document would protect Canada's claim over the viruses, assuming they had been patented through the Budapest Treaty deposit, an internationally recognized system for patenting intentions involving microorganisms.

"If China was leveraging these scientists in Canada to gain access to a potentially valuable pathogen or to elements of a virus without having to license the patent . . . it makes sense with the idea of China

trying to gain access to valuable IP without paying for it," says Leah West, an expert in national security law at the Norman Paterson School of International Affairs, in an interview with CBC News.

China agreed to the Biological Weapons Convention in 1984, but both academics and government agencies have recently asserted that the country is a world leader in bio-weapon production, according to the Edmonton Journal.

"I would say this Canadian 'contribution' might likely be counterproductive. I think the Chinese activities . . . are highly suspicious, in terms of exploring [at least] those viruses as BW [biological warfare] agents," says Dany Shoham, a biological and chemical warfare expert at Israel's Bar-Ilan University, in an interview with the Edmonton Journal.

"Frankly, if it's already in China, cat's out of the bag," adds China intellectual property expert Mark Cohen in an interview with the Winnipeg Free Press. "They're probably culturing it already." The March shipment took place during a dispute between the US and China, which led to the arrest of an executive of Huawei Technologies and the later detainment of two Canadians in China, according to the Winnipeg Free Press. Given the tension between the two countries, Chinese-Canadian researchers and academics are starting to worry they may be singled out and targeted, says Jia Wang, deputy director of the University of Alberta's China Institute, in an interview with CBC News. "As China observers, we'd like to perhaps gently remind people not to jump into any conclusions too quickly."

Nicoletta Lanese is an intern at The Scientist. Email her at nlanese@the-scientist.com.

BIO-WARFARE EXPERTS QUESTION WHY CANADA WAS SENDING LETHAL VIRUSES TO CHINA

'I think the Chinese activities … are highly suspicious,' one expert said, after it was revealed a Winnipeg lab sent samples of Ebola and henipavirus to China

By Tom Blackwell. The National Post.

More here: https://nationalpost.com/health/bio-warfare-experts-question-why-canada-was-sending-lethal-viruses-to-china

August 8th 2019

In a table-top pandemic exercise at Johns Hopkins University last year, **a pathogen based on the emerging Nipah virus was released by fictional extremists, killing 150 million people**. *A less apocalyptic*

scenario mapped out by a blue-ribbon U.S. panel envisioned Nipah being dispersed by terrorists and claiming over 6,000 American lives.

Scientists from Canada's National Microbiology Laboratory (NML) have also said the highly lethal bug is a potential bio-weapon. But this March that same lab shipped samples of the henipavirus family and of Ebola to China, which has long been suspected of running a secretive biological warfare (BW) program. *China strongly denies it makes germ weapons, and Canadian officials say the shipment was part of its efforts to support public-health research worldwide.* ***Sharing of such samples internationally is relatively standard practice. But some experts are raising questions about the March transfer, which appears to be at the centre of a shadowy RCMP investigation and dismissal of a top scientist at the Winnipeg-based NML.***

"I would say this Canadian 'contribution' might likely be counterproductive," said Dany Shoham, a biological and chemical warfare expert at Israel's Bar-Ilan University. "I think the Chinese activities ... are highly suspicious, in terms of exploring (at least) those viruses as BW agents."

James Giordano, a neurology professor at Georgetown University and senior fellow in biowarfare at the U.S. Special Operations Command, said it's worrisome on a few fronts.

China's growing investment in bio-science, looser ethics around gene-editing and other cutting-edge technology and integration between government and academia raise the spectre of such pathogens being weaponized, *he said.*

That could mean an offensive agent, or a modified germ let loose by proxies, for which only China has the treatment or vaccine, said Giordano, co-head of Georgetown's Brain Science and Global Law and Policy Program. ***"This is not warfare, per se," he said. "But what it's doing is leveraging the capability to act as global saviour, which then creates various levels of macro and micro economic and bio-power dependencies."***

Asked if the possibility of the Canadian germs being diverted into a Chinese weapons program is connected to other upheaval at the microbiology lab, Public Health Agency of Canada spokeswoman Anna Maddison said this week the agency "continues to look into the administrative matter." The agency divulged last week that it sent samples of Ebola and henipavirus — which includes Nipah and the related Hendra — to China in March. It was meant for virus research, part of the agency's mission to back international public-health research, a spokesman said.

Last month, an acclaimed NML scientist — Xiangguo Qiu — was reportedly escorted out of the lab along with her husband, another biologist, and members of her research team. The agency said it was investigating an "administrative issue," and had referred a possible policy breach to the RCMP. Little more has been said about the affair. **China has been a signatory to the Biological Weapons Convention since 1984, and has repeatedly insisted it is abiding by the treaty that bans developing bio-weapons. But suspicions have persisted, with the U.S. State Department and other agencies stating publicly as recently as 2009 that they believe China has offensive biological agents.** *Though no details have appeared in the open literature,* **China is "commonly considered to have an active biological warfare program,"** *says the Federation of American Scientists. An official with the U.S. Army Medical Research Institute of Chemical Defence charged last month* **China is the world leader in toxin "threats."**

In a 2015 academic paper, Shoham – of Bar-Ilan's Begin-Sadat Center for Strategic Studies – asserts that **more than 40 Chinese facilities are involved in bio-weapon production. China's Academy of Military Medical Sciences actually developed an Ebola drug – called JK-05 — but little has been divulged about it or the defence facility's possession of the virus, prompting speculation its Ebola cells are part of China's bio-warfare arsenal,** *Shoham told the National Post.*

Ebola is classified as a "category A" bioterrorism agent by the U.S. Centers for Disease Control and Prevention, meaning it could be easily transmitted from person to person, would result in high death rates and "might cause panic." The CDC lists Nipah as a category C substance, a deadly emerging pathogen that could be engineered for mass dissemination.

Nipah, which was first seen in Malaysia in 1998, has caused a series of outbreaks across east and south Asia, with death rates mostly over 50 per cent, and as high as 100 per cent, according to World Health Organization figures. *It can cause encephalitis, an often-fatal brain swelling, and has no known treatment or vaccine.* **The Johns Hopkins exercise — called Clade X — involved a version of Nipah modified to be more easily passed between people.**

America's Blue Ribbon Study Panel on Biodefence prefaced its 2015 report with a scenario involving the intentional release of Nipah by aerosol spray. China's extensive and controversial use of CRISPR gene-editing and related technology makes it conceivable the country could bio-engineer germs like Nipah to make them even more dangerous, Giordano said.

CANADIAN EBOLA DRUG INVENTORS WORKED WITH CHINESE FIRM BUT IT WAS ABOUT SAVING LIVES, TOP BIOLOGIST SAYS

It's unlikely any aspect of the National Microbiology Laboratory's work is being traded to China, since treating relatively rare diseases is far from lucrative

By Tom Blackwell. The National Post.

More here: https://nationalpost.com/news/XXXanadian-ebola-drug-inventors-worked-with-chinese-firm-but-it-was-about-saving-lives-top-biologist-says

July 17th 2019

A Canadian researcher who was suddenly dismissed from a federal lab recently worked with a Chinese company that copied a breakthrough Ebola drug she helped discover. But it was definitely not a case of economic espionage, says the leading biologist who spearheaded development of the medicine. Gary Kobinger said both he and Xiangguo Qiu co-operated with MabWorks while they were at Winnipeg's National Microbiology Laboratory (NML). The Beijing firm was up-front about what it had done – despite the drug being under patent – and probably saved lives by increasing production of the experimental product at its own cost, he said. Kobinger urged the federal government to be more transparent about the reasons for Qiu's removal from the Winnipeg lab, and squelch speculation that has focused largely on the researcher's ties to her native China.

It's unlikely any aspect of NML's work is being traded to that country, since treating relatively rare diseases like Ebola is far from lucrative, and their research is all published openly, anyway. "The angle that is coming out of this I think is unfortunate. This angle of paranoia, that people are stealing and this and that," said Kobinger, who left the lab three years ago to assume a Canada research chair at the University of Laval. "It's a bit sad, it's kind of politicizing science, because of tensions between two countries." Kobinger said the role of the lab – which has built a stellar international reputation – was hazy when he was there, and that could be behind Qiu's troubles. "A lot of people in government thought it was not good that NML was doing research. And some other people were thrilled about it," he recalled. "This is where I could see a lot of misunderstandings and problems ... The government is good at making new policies and it's frequent that a new policy may contradict another one."

An unconfirmed report by CBC says that Qiu, her husband Keding Cheng – also a biologist at the NML – and her entire research team of students, were escorted from the facility July 5. The Public Health Agency of Canada has said only that it is looking into an "administrative matter," and advised the RCMP on May 24 of "possible policy breaches" at the lab. The University of Manitoba said it suspended Qiu's appointment as an unpaid adjunct professor "pending an RCMP investigation."

Under Kobinger's leadership, the pair developed "monoclonal antibodies" that have shown promise against deadly Ebola. Their discovery comprises two of three elements in Zmapp, a drug being developed by a California company, Mapp Biopharmaceutical Inc. It has yet to receive regulatory approval.

Though no evidence has emerged of any wrongdoing by Qiu, U.S. authorities have warned repeatedly lately about the danger of scientists with Chinese connections helping Beijing illegally acquire intellectual property and trade secrets. Kobinger said he does not believe his former colleague would do anything of the sort, despite their co-operating with Beijing's MabWorks after it admitted to using data posted online in patents to copy the treatment. In fact, the company ended up collaborating both with the Canadian researchers and Mapp Biopharmaceutical, he said. "When the guy called me, I remember very well, he was nervous and he said, 'You know we took the sequences online, we just wanted to see if we could make them,' " recalled Kobinger. "They were (later) just giving the stuff away for free ... So I think an argument could be made that lives were saved by this company that decided to make some product when we didn't have enough in North America. It's great what they did."

For now, he said, the sudden ejection of Qiu from the Canadian lab will only cause uncertainty among those who work in the field. "I think this is going to be a chill on the scientific community," said the biologist "I think it's not good for government scientists, I don't think it's good for science in general."

INDICTED MCGILL PROFESSOR WAS CAUGHT IN BROAD, CONTROVERSIAL U.S. DRAGNET OF CHINESE-BACKGROUND SCIENTISTS

Some prominent critics suggest America's trade war with China has propelled police on a witch hunt against east-Asian researchers

By Tom Blackwell. The National Post.

More here: https://nationalpost.com/news/indicted-mcgill-professor-was-caught-in-broad-controversial-u-s-dragnet-of-chinese-background-scientists
July 12th 2019

The U.S. criminal indictment against Canadian Ishiang Shih grabs attention. It is not everyday, after all, that a professor at a prestigious university is charged with illegally exporting advanced technology to China. But the now-retired McGill faculty member is just one among numerous scientists of Chinese descent caught up recently in a controversial American dragnet, its goal to combat economic espionage by Beijing.

Researchers for private companies and universities have been charged with various crimes, as well as non-Chinese intelligence agents and civil servants. Others have been fired summarily. One Washington, D.C. lawyer says he represents three-dozen Chinese-American scientists who have been charged or put under suspicion by federal authorities. *They now feel unfairly scrutinized, stigmatized and on edge – because of their Chinese ethnicity alone.* ***The U.S. Justice Department, which concentrated its efforts on the issue by launching a new "China Initiative" last year, says it's trying to combat Beijing's well-documented campaign to acquire foreign technological secrets by any means****.*

Some prominent critics, however, suggest America's trade war with China has propelled police on a witch hunt against east-Asian researchers. "In managing these risks, we must take great care not to create a toxic atmosphere of unfounded suspicion and fear," Massachusetts Institute of Technology president Rafael Reif wrote in an open letter last month. "Yet faculty members, post-docs, research staff and students tell me that, in their dealings with government agencies, they now feel unfairly scrutinized, stigmatized and on edge – because of their Chinese ethnicity alone."

A Chinese American academic who was earlier charged with sending secrets to China – then cleared because agents misunderstood the nature of his work – is suing the U.S. government, helped by the American Civil Liberties Union.

"I think what is wrong is to single out a particular ethnic group for surveillance and prosecution," Xiaoxing Xi, the former physics department chair at Philadelphia's Temple University, said in an interview Thursday. "That is racial profiling."

In Canada, meanwhile, the RCMP says it has no country-specific investigation program, while universities report they are working with

China to their "mutual benefit." Yet there is certainly widespread consensus that China often uses illegal methods to acquire technology developed elsewhere, for military use or to give domestic companies a competitive leg-up.

Trump administration officials have been blunt in describing the threat they perceive from the research community. FBI offices across the U.S. see evidence China uses "non-traditional collectors" of such intelligence, including Chinese students, professors and scientists, FBI Director Christopher Wray told a congressional hearing last year. "I think the level of naivete on the part of the academic sector about this creates its own issues," he said. "They're exploiting the very open research and development environment that we have, which we all revere, but they're taking advantage of it." *They're exploiting the very open research and development environment that we have.*

Montreal's Shih was indicted last year along with brother Yi-Chi – a fellow electrical engineer who has worked at UCLA – with conspiring to send advanced computer chips to China, contrary to export restrictions. Yi-Chi was convicted recently, and a source said the U.S. has asked Canada to extradite Ishiang, who retired from McGill last year. But the California-based brother's lawyer said the case was a "tragic" miscarriage of justice that saw the jury deprived of key evidence. Yi-Chi had designed the chip himself, and the American company whose design tools he used actually has a large operation – and half its workforce – in China.

Broader concerns are being raised about the idea of going after researchers of one race, and the nature of many of the prosecutions to date. Peter Zeidenberg, a Washington, D.C. lawyer who represented Xi, said agents have completely misconstrued the science and reached wrong conclusions in a "very large percentage" of the three-dozen or so such cases he's taken on.

"They do not understand what is going on and they're assuming the worst," he told a recent panel at New York City's China Institute. "It's becoming a criminalization based on a paranoia."

Charges were dropped against Xi when police acknowledged the physicist had not sent to China the type of technology they claimed he had. Even if he had done so, says Xi, that science is publicly available – not a secret. Regardless, he said the 2015 prosecution has had a devastating effect, with his federal grants almost disappearing and the number of students and post-doctoral fellows on his research team shrinking to three from 15. "The impact on my career is huge," he said.

And now, "I worry constantly that the government will twist something I do in order to lay charges."

In Canada, meanwhile, there is little evidence security agencies have taken a pro-active approach to any China threat on campuses. The RCMP "does not have an investigative unit targeting any particular foreign entity," said Cpl. Caroline Duval, a spokeswoman for the force. And a spokeswoman for Canadian universities' umbrella group said she is aware of no warnings of the type reportedly issued by American security agencies to colleges about economic espionage and China. "Many universities have very productive research relationships with China that are mutually beneficial," added Universities Canada official Alison Evans by email. Others were more ambiguous.

At McGill, 15 personnel met with Canadian Security Intelligence Service officials last December about "potential issues surrounding collaborations with companies outside of Canada," said spokesman Vincent Campbell Allaire. He wouldn't elaborate or say if those issues involved China. The University of Toronto said only that it has heard from the government about "general security issues" but has received no requests "regarding specific individuals"

CHINA, CHINA, CHINA

As I write, the Novel Coronavirus/Covid-19 has affected 213 countries, infected 5,552,716 people with over 2 million recovering, killed 348,095 people, and those are only the figures that are known and are rising constantly, which is likely a small percentage of the global population since testing is only in the toddler stage, with many like myself having a "mysterious" illness long before the Coronavirus release was ever reported by China.

I've always been curious and sought out the unknown. After finishing school, curiosity took on a whole new meaning. Sometimes I spend hours into days searching the internet, including the dark web, for all types of information, especially that pertaining to the humanities and the human condition. One day in early October 2019 I came across a video of a Chinese doctor issuing a warning about a viral outbreak that was surging in Wuhan, China.

He stated that a deadly biological agent had "gotten away" from the lab where he worked many weeks earlier and was infecting people in the area at an increasingly alarming rate, much faster than even its creators had predicted. He went on to say he believed the virus was being created as a biological warfare agent like SARS and MERS had been, but it was going to be much more virulent and successful. Its test run was going to be Hong Kong and Taiwan once a vaccine to stop/control it was created because The Party wanted them back under its control.

Unfortunately, the screen went black in the middle of a sentence and I never heard the full video. I tried to bring the video back up but there was nothing to find. I didn't think that much of it since China is a world away from my farm and I was used to finding dire warnings about all types of apocalyptic events posted by conspiracy theorists and doomsday soothsayers that were pulled by the powers that be, so I simply moved on.

At 3am on December 26th, 2019 I was wakened by a vicious fit of coughing. Having COPD that encompasses emphysema, chronic bronchitis, and asthma this was nothing new. I used my rescue inhaler and waited for the cough to subside. When I was still coughing relentlessly at 7:30am I called my doctor. They got me in a few hours later. I had no fever or any other symptoms other than the cough. I was prescribed a 10-day ZPac to head off any possible respiratory infections, some strong cough syrup, and sent home. The cough syrup would knock me out for a few hours, but the cough never even slowed down.

Still coughing as relentlessly as day one I went to the emergency room on January 2nd, 2020. The ER doctor did a chest X-ray that showed the usual disaster area my lungs are with a new twist, a mass in my right Suprahilar. He had me take 60mg of prednisone and do a fifteen-minute albuterol breathing treatment. I was sent home with five days of prednisone, another type of cough syrup, an order for a CT scan, and advice to use my nebulizer twice a day. His "diagnosis" was that his best guess was the mass was either an infiltrant or a spot of pneumonia, but since I had no other symptoms, we'd have to wait for the CT scan results to know what was causing the cough. Being no stranger to COPD exacerbations I wondered if this was just the worst I'd ever had, but he didn't think so since exacerbations aren't quite so relentless and only last a few hours or days, not a week.

The week between the ER visit and the CT scan wasn't quite so treacherous, possibly due to the prednisone, the Z-pack, and the increased use of the nebulizer. A couple days before the scan I coughed up a rather large glob of something while doing dishes one evening. It didn't affect the cough, but I could breathe a little better. When I returned to my doctor's office for the results of the CT scan there was no mass to be found, but the cough had become as relentless as ever as soon as I finished the prednisone. I went home with another type of cough syrup, with no better luck.

In the following weeks I was in and out of the doctor's office so much we joked I should have a monogramed cushion on a chair in the waiting room. The cough was as relentless as always and I was getting worn down to a nub from it, and the lack of sleep it caused. I don't know exactly when it stopped, but I actually slept the night of February 1st/2nd. The coughing stopped just as abruptly as it started sometime during the night.

It took six weeks of sleeping fourteen to sixteen hours a night to begin to feel human again. In the meantime, the Novel Coronavirus outbreak had broken in the news and "stay at home" orders were being discussed in daily pressers by the governor and The Donald. Since I had never been given any type of diagnosis other than "your guess is as good as mine" by my doctor, I was still under the impression that it had been a record-breaking COPD exacerbation although a good friend stated she wasn't so sure about that a few times. She speculated several times that it could've been Covid-19, but being as hard-headed as I am, I stuck with the exacerbation theory, for a little while longer anyway.

Update – a recent antibody test was negative, no exposure, not to the Coronavirus the test was engineered for anyway.

Once I got back on my feet and really started paying attention to the news and got up to speed my friend in Edmonton and I had quite a few conversations about the outbreak. It was during one such conversation that she told me about Chinese virologists working at a lab in Winnipeg sending viruses to China and being expelled by the RCMP because the viruses sent were alleged biological agents. That began my research into the origins of the Novel Coronavirus. The previous articles are just a few examples of what I uncovered. There are many more articles linked to the ones I provided; the ones I choose to include in this work contain the most comprehensive information that pertains to the point of this portion of the narrative.

Enough about my experience, let's get to the point. As attested to by the previous articles the first inkling the U.S. "intelligence community" (intelligence is a misnomer, these idiotic bureaucrats are as ideologically corrupt, morally bankrupt, and incompetent as their chairman) led by Congressman Adam Schiff (Dem. – Cal.) had that biological agents were being created in their backyard was in late March of 2019. However, at that time the only information Schiff was concerned with was dirt on Trump's alleged collusion with Russia during the 2016 election. The information was ignored and if Trump was briefed on it at all he dismissed it as "fake news" or just another hoax perpetrated by "shifty Schiff" and his socialist cronies in congress.

July 2019 was the next warning the U.S. had about biological agents being created in their backyard. It was then that four Chinese virologists working in a Winnipeg lab were expelled from Canada by the RCMP after an investigation into their activities, especially their shipping Ebola and Nipah viruses, both determined to be biological agents, to a lab in Wuhan, China. It's now known they took a third virus with them, Coronavirus (I wonder if they were working on it in Canada so they could set it loose on the North American continent without affecting China?).

Again, the "intelligence community" was far more concerned with the Mueller Report's lack of collusion findings (it's recently come to light that the chairman of Trump's campaign team, Paul Manafort, was funneling information to Russian Intelligence officer, Konstantin Kilimnik throughout the campaign) and a congratulatory phone call Trump had with the new Ukrainian President, Volodymyr Zelensky, on July 25th where he asked for help investigating Ukrainian corruption.

Schiff assumed it was Burisma, an extremely corrupt Ukrainian natural gas company that employed Joe Biden's son, Hunter, from 2014 to 2019, because Joe Biden was one of the Democratic candidates for the 2020 election. Again, the information was ignored. If Trump was briefed at all he again dismissed it as "fake news," a "socialist hoax," or ignored it because it wasn't about him.

The political and media circus that ensued after Adam Schiff initiated an investigation against Trump after a secret, never to be named, whistleblower, whom I suspect never existed, claimed they heard Trump attempt to extort a quid pro quo corruption investigation for $4million in aid out of Zelensky during the call, even though both Zelensky and Trump denied it, there was no specific mention of Burisma or Biden, nor was there anything more than 'hey, do me a favor' in the transcript of the call.

This "investigation" became a circus unto itself after Schiff's alleged witnesses denied any wrongdoing by Trump in open hearings. Schiff then held 'secret hearings' (more like coercion/coaching sessions) in a sub-basement of congress, which resulted in all the witnesses recanting their original testimonies and claiming they heard what they "assumed" was a quid pro quo deal being made during the phone call. The sham resulted in an impeachment hearing, which of course resulted in a trial and ultimately the senate exonerating Trump in early December.

From August 2019 to January 2020 some of the squabbling three-year-olds that claim to be our "leaders" and Democratic candidates for president condemned Trump and occasionally each other as they attempted to steer the moronic majority in their favor. None more so than Joe Biden, probably one of the dumbest politicians ever, whose only talent and experience for nearly fifty years has been opening his idiotic mouth, inserting his foot up to the knee, and backpedaling after being called on his gaffs and blatant hypocrisy.

Speaking of Biden's stupidity and hypocrisy. He constantly condemned Trump for the alleged quid pro quo with Zelensky after doing the exact same thing. Below is the link to a video of Biden on the dais at a 2018 Council on Foreign Relations meeting bragging about withholding $1billion in aid to Ukraine in 2016 if the then prosecutor general, Viktor Shokin, who was investigating Burisma, wasn't fired immediately. He was fired the next day; Burisma was never investigated; Hunter Biden then worked there for three more years for an enormous salary even though he had no knowledge of energy production or Ukrainian law.

According to 'fact check' the difference between Biden's actions and Trump's is Biden was following standard procedure and Trump was doing it strictly for the sake of digging up dirt on Biden due to the 2020 election, which he may've been, but he never mentioned his motive during the call, it was just assumed by Adam Schiff who in turn coerced his 'witnesses' into stating it during the secret basement hearings.

Watch "VP JOE BIDEN ON CFR QUID PRO QUO M NNN" on YouTube
https://www.youtube.com/watch?v=vCSF3reVr10&feature=youtu.be

When news of the Novel Coronavirus "outbreak" in China finally surfaced in January, China initially claimed it came from eating bats sold in a wet market in Wuhan, it was under control, and there was no possibility of human to human transmission. However, the first cases had no connection to the market and as the virus spread like wildfire in China it was evident they were lying about its transmission. Even though he was briefed on it in November, Trump insisted it was just another "socialist hoax" like "Russia, Russia, Russia" and "Ukraine, Ukraine, Ukraine" and ignored all the warnings. Meanwhile infected Chinese were flying all over the world for business and pleasure, ultimately spreading the virus to 213 countries.

From the end of December to March Trump categorically denied that Covid-19 was anything more than a hoax while the infection and death rates climbed around the world and in the U.S.… However, he did suspend all Chinese travel to the U.S. in late February while infected Europeans and Americans returning from Europe continued to flood in.

Caught with their pants down the CDC, WHO, and other health organizations scrambled to put countermeasures in place, which ended up being closing countries, banning travel, issuing "stay at home", mask wearing, "social distancing," and business lockdown orders to name the most prevalent.

It wasn't until the first few weeks of March that Trump began changing his tune, which initially was not to worry, the virus would just make its way through the population and miraculously disappear with little affect. It did everything but and Trump in his infinite stupidity assumed he could deny, bully, and lie his way through it and no one would be the wiser.

By the end of March, Trump was claiming his was the best response in the world and the U.S. was leading the way in testing, treating, and providing personal protective equipment for the medical staff involved in attempting to arrest the virus and treat the sick and dying, while the exact opposite was true. Fact is, in 2018 at Trump's direction, John Bolton dismantled all the pandemic protocols and PPE stock piles put in place by George W. Bush while Trump scrapped the Novel Coronavirus Pandemic Plan Obama/Biden instituted in 2016 (which begs the question, how did Obama/Biden know we'd be hit by a Coronavirus pandemic? It was claimed to just be a coincidence). Additionally, the U.S. leads the world in infection and death rates.

As the outbreak was gaining momentum someone asked me if I thought it was yet another ploy to further divide the population which is already divided along so many lines some people even hate themselves. I said I didn't think so, but what I've found is it created a lot of suspicion and animosity between some mask wearers and others, like myself, that can't wear them due to medical conditions. With some of them fleeing the area as if I were on fire at the sight of my masklessness, or "ordering" me to wear a mask as if they possessed some type of authority to do so and complaining to store personnel when I refused or ignored them.

It was extremely surreal to walk through a Lowes one day and find myself in a scene from any one of the 'pandemic/totalitarian takeover' movies that have been made over the years. As I walked down a main isle populated by masked people visibly distancing themselves from each other while "wear your mask, maintain social distancing, and wash your hands frequently" public safety announcements droned over the loudspeaker every few minutes I felt as if I were in a Déjà vu. It's also pretty irritating when a busybody interrupts a conversation with a friend to tell us we should be six feet apart.

"NEVER LET A CRISIS GO TO WASTE." – Saul Alinsky

After reading Agenda 21, witnessing China's totalitarian 5G surveillance state activities pre, during, and post pandemic, reading many of the elite's manifestos, and seeing all the "pandemic protection" technologies about to be instituted globally I can tell you that this pandemic will be used to acclimate "free" societies to being locked down; surveilled 24/7/365 with extremely invasive infrared facial recognition cameras that report elevated body temperatures and fevers to an algorithmically governed system; being constantly tracked by contact tracing technologies surreptitiously loaded into everyone's smart phone and built into standalone machines connected to the burgeoning 5G surveillance grid that identifies everyone a person makes any kind of contact with during their day to day activities. Tracking all subsequent contacts under the guise of "safety, protection, and convenience" so they can be "quarantined"/locked down as they were in China, if infected. The mask wearing will accustom people to vilifying and reporting 'others' that aren't "following the rules" to persons of authority, basically creating a society of snitches because "see something say something" hasn't worked nearly as well as projected.

As the virus circumnavigated the globe, China's initial denial of the virus in order to hoard the PPE it manufactured; vague, shifting, spurious statistics (including declaring the dead as cured); subsequent silence once its actions, inactions, lies (no human to human transfer and many others) became apparent. Their refusal to supply the virus's genome for several months so a vaccine could be made (done so they could return it to its original state), as well as its well-known domination by any means agenda only made the rest of the world more suspicious.

They then resorted to accusations that the virus was created in America and shipped to China with the intention of ruining its economy and manufacturing industry after expelling the western investigative journalists that were reporting its activities and tactics to the rest of the world. For example, shipping all its defective PPE to hard hit countries like Italy in an effort to project the image of cooperation, global citizenship, and beneficence while secretly hoarding all the good PPE allowing the pandemic to spread further and faster, forcibly rounding up anyone that violated the lockdown, and the rendition of doctors that spoke out.

FUTURE SHOCK

I may be totally wrong, and I honestly hope I am. I may be able to predict how this pandemic is going to play out moving forward, though. Given that Covid-19 is a synthetic biological agent (which, by the way, American virologists categorically deny while supporting the animal to human jump theory wholeheartedly) that behaves like no other virus known to man due to the four synthetic amino acids that were spliced into its DNA. The purpose of which was to make it more virulent, transmit rapidly, mutate rapidly, environmentally resistant, and alter its manifestation in various age groups/races/areas we will never "get it under control," at least not until its architects come forward, if they haven't been executed, with its blueprint.

Until that time, it will run rampant through the population with constantly increasing vectors, transmission strength and distances. It will mutate rapidly when confronted by a vaccine and the temporary soft immunity it provides; rampage through the population irrespective of environmental temperature or moisture levels, and manifest in ever increasingly diverse manners. Eventually it will be strong enough to become airborne on the prevailing winds like the 800 billion other innocuous viruses and bacteria that travel the world daily, especially with the delusionary, Trump, claiming it's all but gone and insisting everything must be opened up now or face governmental sanctions.

Only those with hard immunity will survive long enough to generate a herd immunity, if that's at all possible due to its mutation ability; by the dawn of 2026 we won't even recognize what's left of this world, not solely due to this virus either. Many more disasters, viral, bacterial (superbugs), natural, and manmade are on the horizon; life will be an unimaginable ordeal as the planet repels us while society exterminates itself.

Today, Wednesday, September 9th, 2020, as I prepare to publish this work there are 27,764,017 cases of Covid-19 globally with 19,848,805 recoveries and 902,356 deaths. In the U.S. there are 6,514,376 cases with 3,797,173 recoveries and 194,037 deaths. According to Trump "we're rounding the corner." September 10th, 2020, Trump finally admitted to lying to Americans about the seriousness of Covid-19 with the excuse he didn't want to create a panic.

END THE INSANITY OF RELIGION

"FUNDAMENTALLY, MY TERM *IMMORALIST* INVOLVES TWO NEGATIONS. FOR ONE I NEGATE A TYPE OF MAN THAT HAS SO FAR BEEN CONSIDERED SUPREME: THE GOOD, THE BENEVOLENT, THE BENEFICENT. AND THEN I NEGATE A TYPE OF MORALITY THAT HAS BECOME AS PREVALENT AND PREDOMINANT AS MORALITY ITSELF – THE MORALITY OF DECADENCE OR, MORE CONCRETELY, *CHRISTIAN* MORALITY." – Freidrich Nietzsche, *Ecce Homo, Why I Am A Destiny, sec. 4*

"BUNCH TOGETHER A GROUP OF PEOPLE DELIBERATELY CHOSEN FOR STRONG RELIGIOUS FEELINGS, AND YOU HAVE A PRACTICAL GUARANTEE OF DARK MORBIDITIES EXPRESSED IN CRIME, PERVERSION, AND INSANITY." – H.P. Lovecraft

"TRULY, THEIR SAVIORS THEMSELVES DID NOT COME FROM FREEDOM AND FREEDOM'S SEVENTH HEAVEN! TRULY, THEY THEMSELVES HAVE NEVER WALKED ON THE CARPETS OF KNOWLEDGE! THE SPIRIT OF THOSE SAVIORS CONSISTED OF EMPTINESS; BUT INTO EVERY GAP THEY PUT THEIR DELUSION, THEIR STOPGAP, WHICH THEY CALLED GOD." – Freidrich Nietzsche, *Thus Spoke Zarathustra*

"BUT WHAT IS THE GOOD OF STILL SOOTHING THE DELICATE EARS OF OUR MODERN EFFEMINATES? WHAT IS THE GOOD *ON OUR SIDE* OF BUDGING ONE SINGLE INCH BEFORE THEIR VERBAL PECKSNIFFIANISM (**hypocritical piety**)? FOR US PSYCHOLOGISTS TO DO THAT WOULD BE AT ONCE *PRACTICAL PECKSNIFFIANISM,* APART FROM THE FACT OF IT'S NAUSEATING US. THE *GOOD TASTE* (OTHERS MIGHT SAY, THE RIGHTEOUSNESS) OF A PSYCHOLOGIST NOWADAYS CONSISTS, IF AT ALL, IN COMBATING THE SHAMEFULLY MORALISED LANGUAGE WITH WHICH ALL MODERN JUDGEMENTS ON MEN AND THINGS ARE SMEARED." – Freidrich Nietzsche, *The Genealogy of Morals*

"The Carrot and the Stick" has been a favorite tactic of rulers since ancient times and religion is the most amazing version ever conceived. The dogmatized myth of an imaginary heaven or hell diametric opposition is the most influential "carrot and stick" ever created by the religious elite. Once perfected, it lulled the ignorant masses into total compliance with their rulers' every whim and is still doing so twenty-three centuries later.

If I told you lightning and thunder was the result of a giant man on top of a mountain banging two big rocks together because he was mad about something I did, you'd tell me I was crazy. However, if I told you there was an omnipresent, omnipotent, invisible man that ruled an invisible kingdom somewhere above the clouds that impregnated a Lebanese woman 2000+ years ago, you and billions of people would agree. Well, the myth of the man in the clouds was the evolutionary product of the myth of the giant with the rocks.

"THE CONCEPT OF "GOD" INVENTED AS A COUNTERCONCEPT OF LIFE – EVERYTHING HARMFUL, POISONOUS, SLANDEROUS, THE WHOLE HOSTILITY UNTO DEATH AGAINST LIFE SYNTHESIZED IN THIS CONCEPT IN A GRUESOME UNITY! THE CONCEPT OF THE "BEYOND" THE "TRUE WORLD" INVENTED IN ORDER TO DEVALUATE THE ONLY WORLD THERE IS – IN ORDER TO RETAIN NO GOAL, NO REASON, NO TASK FOR OUR EARTHLY REALITY! THE CONCEPT OF THE "SOUL," THE "SPIRIT," FINALLY EVEN *IMMORTAL SOUL*," INVENTED IN ORDER TO DESPISE THE BODY, TO MAKE IT SICK, "HOLY"; TO OPPOSE WITH A GHASTLY LEVITY EVERYTHING THAT DESERVES TO BE TAKEN SERIOUSLY IN LIFE, THE QUESTIONS OF NOURISHMENT, ABODE, SPIRITUAL DIET, TREATMENT OF THE SICK, CLEANLINESS, AND WEATHER." – Freidrich Nietzsche, *Ecce Homo*

Prehistoric man's ignorance of the causes of natural events that affected his world like rain, snow, lightning, thunder, wind, earth, sky, water, sun, and moon resulted in the creation of a myriad of imaginary giant men and women that were called by names man assigned them to explain the things he couldn't understand, including why good and bad things happened to him and how he came to be.

The term "God" is a relatively new term in the history of man's spirituality. For thousands of years man invented, named, and worshipped thousands of gods and goddesses that allegedly influenced or controlled every aspect of peoples' lives. There were so many gods that most people chose a few they deemed important for one reason or another and focused on them, giving the others only an occasional passing glance during their festivals.

It wasn't until the polytheistic Romans created and adopted Christianity as their state religion that a term for the one imaginary sky-god came into use. Up until that time the polytheistic Judeans, they stole the components of their new religion from, worshipped two main gods as well as many lesser others. The Canaanites worshipped El and the Israelites worshipped Yahweh or Jehovah (the Mosaic equivalent) as their main gods but had many lesser gods and goddesses they prayed to as well.

"GOD'S ONLY EXCUSE IS THAT HE DOES NOT EXIST." – Stendhal, as quoted by Friedrich Nietzsche, *Ecce Homo, Why I Am So Clever, sec. 3*

"WHAT HAS BEEN THE GREATEST OBJECTION TO EXISTENCE SO FAR? *GOD.*" – Friedrich Nietzsche, *Ecce Homo, Why I Am So Clever, sec.3*

LOOKING FOR GOD IN RELIGIOUS TEXTS IS LIKE LOOKING FOR A DOG IN A POUND. YOU'RE GONNA FIND ONE EVERYWHERE YOU LOOK.

The Romans created a monotheistic mashup of the Judean main gods in their bible and a new messiah myth to support it that took 451 years to rectify and ratify to create their state religion's deity which was initially called Numen in their Latin language; eventually becoming God when the Germans and English got ahold of it as the religion spread throughout what was once the Roman Empire….

""GOD HIMSELF CANNOT EXIST WITHOUT WISE MEN" – LUTHER SAID, AND WAS RIGHT. BUT "GOD CAN EXIST EVEN LESS WITHOUT UNWISE MEN" – THAT GOOD OLD LUTHER DID NOT SAY." – Friedrich Nietzsche, *The Gay Science*

After creating their new deity, prophet, and religion Roman Legionnaires traveled the entire western world exterminating all the polytheistic religions and the competing monotheistic religions, plundering their temples, stealing their religious documents and secreting them in the catacombs beneath what's now the Vatican. Their greatest achievement in that holy war being the final sacking and burning of the Library of Alexandria, Egypt, where the religious documents and the history of every religion and civilization was stored. By the sixth century A.D. El was forgotten and Judeans, Christians, and Muslims worshipped Yahweh/Jehovah with Muslims calling him, Allah….

"THE CHRISTIAN RESOLVE TO FIND THE WORLD UGLY AND BAD HAS MADE THE WORLD UGLY AND BAD." – Friedrich Nietzsche, *The Gay Science*

It was during the Axial Age, or the Age of Enlightenment (600BC to 300BC), that emperors and kings discovered the use of religion as the perfect control mechanism of the people. Initially religions were considered a burden by emperors and kings when polytheism was the norm due to the large number of gods, goddesses, religious sects that followed them, and their constant squabbling. To show any preference to any of them resulted in uprisings by the others.

However, when monotheism entered the picture via Zoroastrianism with its one god in heaven and his antagonist in hell it quickly became the epitome of the 'carrot and stick' control tactic all rolled up in one neat package. If you obeyed the emperor, or king, your eternal reward was heaven when you died, if you didn't, hell was your eternal punishment for disobedience upon your demise. With priests reminding the population of that dogma daily and weekly, once difficult populations became easier to control almost overnight.

"IN PLACE OF HEALTH, "SALVATION OF THE SOUL" – THAT IS THE *FOLIE CIRCULAIRE* (**manic-depressive insanity**) BETWEEN PENTITENTIAL CONVULSIONS AND HYSTERIA ABOUT REDEMPTION. THE CONCEPT OF "SIN" INVENTED ALONG WITH THE TORTURE INSTRUMENT THAT BELONGS TO IT, THE CONCEPT OF "FREE WILL," IN ORDER TO CONFUSE THE INSTINCTS, TO MAKE MISTRUST OF THE INSTINCTS SECOND NATURE. IN THE CONCEPT OF "SELFLESS," THE "SELF-DENIER," THE DESTINCTIVE SIGN OF DECADENCE, FEELING ATTRACTED BY WHAT IS HARMFUL, BEING UNABLE TO FIND ANY LONGER WHAT PROFITS ONE, SELF-DESTRUCTION IS TURNED INTO THE SIGN OF VALUE ITSELF, INTO "DUTY," INTO "HOLINESS," INTO WHAT IS "DIVINE" IN MAN." – Freidrich Nietzsche, *Ecce Homo*

"GOD IS A GROSS ANSWER, AN INDELICACY AGAINST US THINKERS – AT BOTTOM MERELY A GROSS PROHIBITION FOR US: YOU SHALL NOT THINK!" – Friedrich Nietzsche, *Ecce Homo, Why I am So Clever, sec. 1*

Although there have been many guesstimations as to the numbers of people killed in wars over whose imaginary god is the best down through history, an accurate number is illusive due to the lack of documentation and censuses until relatively recent times and the rampantly inaccurate myths and legends about prophets and gods and the wars and conquests fought in their names. Some say it's as low as five million while others claim it's as high as fifteen billion. Whatever the number may be, religious wars are still alive and well today and show no sign of ending anytime soon, in fact they seemed to be escalating until everybody took a Covid-19 break.

"WHAT IS THE SUPREME ENJOYMENT FOR MEN WHO LIVE IN THE STATE OF WAR OF THOSE SMALL, CONTINUALLY ENDANGERED COMMUNITIES WHICH ARE CHARACTERIZED BY THE STRICTEST MORES? IN OTHER WORDS, FOR VIGOROUS, VINDICTIVE, VICIOUS,

SUSPICIOUS SOULS WHO ARE PREPARED FOR WHAT IS MOST TERRIBLE AND HARDENED BY DEPRIVATIONS AND MORES? THE ENJOYMENT OF *CRUELTY*; AND IN THESE CIRCUMSTANCES IT IS EVEN ACCOUNTED AMONG THE *VIRTUES* OF SUCH A SOUL IF IT IS INVENTIVE AND INSATIABLE IN CRUELTY. THE COMMUNITY FEELS REFRESHED BY CRUEL DEEDS, AND CASTS OFF FOR ONCE THE GLOOM OF CONTINUAL ANXIETY AND CAUTION. CRUELTY BELONGS TO THE MOST ANCIENT FESTIVE JOYS OF MANKIND. HENCE ONE SUPPOSES THAT THE *GODS*, TOO, FEEL REFRESHED AND FESTIVE WHEN ONE OFFERS THEM THE SIGHT OF CRUELTY; AND SO, THE IDEA CREEPS INTO THE WORLD THAT *VOLUNTARY SUFFERING*, TORTURE ONE HAS CHOSEN ONESELF, HAS VALUE AND MAKES GOOD SENSE. GRADUALLY THE MORES SHAPE A COMMUNAL PRACTICE IN ACCORDANCE WITH THIS IDEA: ALL EXTRAVAGANT WELL-BEING HENCEFORTH AROUSES SOME MISTRUST, AND ALL HARD AND PAINFUL STATES MORE AND MORE CONFIDENCE. ONE SUPPOSES THAT THE GODS MIGHT LOOK UPON US UNGRACIOUSLY BECAUSE OF OUR HAPPINESS, AND GRACIOUSLY BECAUSE OF OUR SUFFERING–NOT BY ANY MEANS WITH PITY. FOR PITY IS CONSIDERED CONTEMPTIBLE AND UNWORTHY OF A STRONG AND TERRIBLE SOUL. RATHER, GRACIOUSLY, BECAUSE IT DELIGHTS THEM AND PUTS THEM INTO GOOD SPIRITS; FOR THOSE WHO ARE CRUEL ENJOY THE SUPREME TITILLATION OF THE FEELING OF POWER." – Friedrich Nietzsche, *The Dawn*

If mankind hopes to survive it must educate itself to the fact that man created god in his image as a means to control other men and it's worked very, very well so far but it's time to abandon the idiocy of gods and religions in favor of humanity and sanity if humanity is to survive and thrive.

"WHATEVER LIVES LONG IS GRADUALLY SO SATURATED WITH REASON THAT ITS IRRATIONAL ORIGINS BECOME IMPROBABLE. DOES NOT ALMOST EVERY ACCURATE HISTORY OF THE ORIGIN OF SOMETHING SOUND PARADOXICAL AND SACRILEGIOUS TO OUR FEELINGS? DOESN'T THE GOOD HISTORIAN *CONTRADICT* ALL THE TIME? – Friedrich Nietzsche, *The Dawn*

END PSEUDOSPECIATION

"READ FROM A DISTANT STAR, THE MAJISCULE SCRIPT OF OUR EARTHLY EXISTENCE WOULD PERHAPS LEAD TO THE CONCLUSION THAT THE EARTH WAS A DISTINCTIVELY *ASCETIC PLANET*, A NOOK OF DISGRUNTLED, ARROGANT, AND OFFENSIVE CREATURES

FILLED WITH A PROFOUND DISGUST AT THEMSELVES, AT THE
EARTH, AT ALL LIFE, WHO INFLICT AS MUCH PAIN ON
THEMSELVES AS THEY POSSIBLY CAN OUT OF PLEASURE IN
INFLICTING PAIN – WHICH IS PROBABLY THEIR ONLY PLEASURE." –
Friedrich Nietzsche, *On the Genealogy of Morals*

Pseudospeciation is the act of creating an outgroup/other that's easily identified by physical, cultural, geographical, ideological, theological, and/or social attributes. It's the essence of tribism and a necessity in removing the psychological barriers to exterminating one's own kind. Pseudospeciation is practiced by our nearest primate ancestors, chimpanzees, and was practiced by every iteration of humans throughout the evolutionary process.

The fossil record of the earliest humans indicates that humans have engaged in conflict since before they began walking upright and making tools. Many archaeological sites of the earliest iterations of man that contain tool artifacts also contain bashed in skulls and tool/weapon inflicted trauma on fossils, often with the offending axe or weapon in close proximity. It seems that as soon as early man began creating tools, they also began using them on each other during conflicts.

By the time mankind was transitioning to large scale agriculture from hunting and gathering they were also adroit at dividing themselves into ingroups and outgroups (tribes) led by kings and devising methods to readily determine the difference in order to defend their groups from those labeled as intruders. Their settlements became city-states which eventually became nation-states and empires led by kings and emperors, which were basically dictators, that used the tactic of 'creating enemies' to maintain a cohesive population by focusing their energies on repelling those that their leader deemed enemies/others/"barbarians" instead of squabbling among themselves or opposing their ruler.

Today, humanity is divided and subdivided along so many imaginary lines it's impossible to keep track of them all, especially since new ones are created every day. Although we "think" we're civilized and have progressed socially from our ancestor's days of clubbing each other over the head because a ruler told us to, the only real "progress" we've made is drawing more imaginary lines and devising more efficient methods of killing each other from greater distances and in larger numbers in an effort to remove the inhumanity of conflict from view while we're constantly escalating it. We never really got beyond the club; it's just become a myriad of other much more murderous technologies that often insulate us from the atrocities we commit until after the fact.

The very bottomline to pseudospeciation/racism/tribism is that there are only eleven degrees of separation between every human on the planet. Given all the migrations of humans in the past several centuries that number has probably decreased to nine, or even eight, degrees of separation, which means we're all distant cousins no matter how different we appear on the outside and we're getting closer all the time. We should be working with each other not against each other, it's the only way we'll survive.

"WHOEVER LEARNS MUCH UNLEARNS ALL VIOLENT DESIRE." – Freidrich Nietzsche, *Thus Spoke Zarathustra*

Additionally, pseudospeciation is a learned behavior. No one is born hating anyone, in fact, just the opposite. We naturally seek and enjoy human interaction with anyone. From birth, newborns and infants are attracted to smiles and pleasant facial expressions no matter who's making them and display negative reactions to scowls and unpleasant expressions, especially on people they're familiar with. We're taught to hate; it doesn't come naturally. I know I was, but it didn't take because there wasn't any affirming evidence to substantiate my father's hateful epithets. In fact, there were many to repudiate them.

My father was born in Georgia 43 years after the end of the Civil War and had a very meager education but he had a strong back and was a skilled craftsman. He wasn't much for social graces and he was extremely prejudice against anyone that wasn't white. For reasons of his own he hated me from conception and I spent my childhood unsuccessfully trying to get his attention and a kind word from him. For that reason, I paid close attention to what he said and did in order to attempt to emulate him thinking that may be a way to get what I sought. Growing up during the civil rights era, whenever Dr. Martin Luther King Jr. was on TV my dad would declare him and all Blacks troublemakers that should be shipped back to Africa if they wanted rights.

I had a problem with that though. There was only one Black family in the tiny rural Maine town I was raised in, they were all my friends and I caused a hell of a lot more trouble than all the Lewis kids put together.

There was one other Black man in our town. He was a janitor and school bus driver for our school system and one of the nicest people you could meet. We all knew and loved him. It looked like I wasn't gonna gain any points with my dad that way.

Fact is, when I got out in the world and really learned about being human, I couldn't hate another human being because they were different, simply because they weren't. We all want the same things; we just have different ways to attempt to attain them based on the influences of our environments. If we worked together to create a balanced environment and society everything harmful would disappear like morning fog in blazing sunlight.

If we want a better world, we must unify to remove the elite's power over us. They keep us divided in order to maintain their power and the previous things listed in the nullification section are the tools they use to do it. By ending money, religion, nations, states, governments, and pseudospeciation/racism/tribism we end all the elite's power and can then create a balanced matricentric society based on equality and cooperation.

ESTABLISH A SOCIETAL BASELINE
No one gets left behind.
THE PIVOTAL COMPONENT

The following article excerpts have been included to show you that we have the technologies we need to do the things I advocate.

TRANSPARENT SOLAR PANELS COULD HARVEST ENERGY FROM WINDOWS AND EVENTUALLY REPLACE FOSSIL FUELS

By Anthony Cuthbertson.
The full story: http://www.newsweek.com/fossil-fuels-transparent-solar-panels-harvest-energy-windows-msu-691308
Oct 24th 2017

A new generation of see-through solar cell technology could soon be used to harvest the massive energy potential of building and car windows, cell phones as well as other objects with a transparent surface. Scientists at Michigan State University detailed in a paper in the journal Nature Energy how highly transparent solar applications could "nearly meet U.S. electricity demand" and drastically reduce reliance upon fossil fuels. "We will see commercial products become available over the next few years," Richard Lunt, an associate professor of Chemical Engineering and Materials Science at MSU, tells Newsweek. "We are just beginning to hit performance metrics that make sense to scale up."

STANFORD RESEARCHERS DISCOVER A BREAK-THROUGH TO CREATE LOW-COST SOLAR CELLS

Published by Tejas Sharma in Science. For the full article:
https://tecake.in/stanford-researchers-discover-break-create-low-cost-solar-cells/amp
2017

A team of talented scientists from Stanford University situated in Stanford, in Silicon Valley, 20 miles (approximately 30 Km) out of San Jose, California, USA have successfully displayed the usage of nanotechnology. The method to manufacture crystalline silicon (c-Si) thin-film solar cells which are being claimed to be more efficient at capturing solar energy. This discovery can pave a path to a breakthrough in reducing the cost of solar energy production globally.

SCIENTISTS CREATE 'ARTIFICIAL PHOTOSYNTHESIS' TO GENERATE CLEAN ENERGY

By Matthew Loffhagen.

https://www.outerplaces.com/science/item/17946-artificial-photosynthesis-clean-energy

Mar 5th 2018

There's a race going on at the moment in the science world. Various teams around the globe are all competing to be the first to produce a solid, stable form of artificial photosynthesis that functions exactly like the real deal in plants.

Thus, teams like the one headed by Boston College professor Dunwei Wang are rushing to be the first to find a form of artificial photosynthesis that matches up to the organic alternative. Wang's team now believe that they've cracked the formula, thanks to a special catalyst that – in theory at least – should allow their version of photosynthesis a lot more stability.

LOOK, NO LITHIUM! FIRST RECHARGABLE PROTON BATTERY CREATED

Researchers say it's a crucial step towards cheaper and more environmentally-friendly energy storage

By Amy McNeilage.

https://www.theguardian.com/technology/2018/mar/09/look-no-lithium-first-rechargeable-proton-battery-created

Mar 8th 2018

Scientists have created the world's first rechargeable proton battery, a crucial step towards cheaper and more environmentally-friendly energy storage.

While the battery is just a small-scale prototype, it has the potential to be competitive with currently available lithium-ion batteries. The rechargeable battery, created by researchers at RMIT university in Melbourne, uses carbon and water instead of lithium.

The lead researcher Professor John Andrews said that as the world moved towards renewables, there would be a significant need for storage technologies that relied on cheap and abundant materials. "Lithium-ion batteries are great but they rely on ultimately scarce and expensive resources," he said. "Hydro is also a good technology but suitable sites are limited and the cost may be very high. The advantage is we're going to be storing protons in a carbon-based material, which is abundant, and we are getting protons from water which is readily available."

The battery itself produces no carbon emissions and it can store electricity from zero-emissions renewables. Andrews said it could be commercially available within five to 10 years. "When it is commercially available, it would be a competitor to the Tesla Powerwall and then eventually we'd hope we might find applications at the scale of the huge Tesla battery [in South Australia] and even larger."

WIND POWER FOR YOUR HOME

The Wind Energy Foundation.

The full story: http://windenergyfoundation.org/wind-at-work/wind-consumers/wind-power-your-home/

For consumers wanting to generate their own green power, installing a small wind turbine may be an option. Small wind turbines are electric generators that use the energy of the wind to produce clean, emissions-free power for individual homes, farms, and small businesses. With this simple and increasingly popular technology, individuals can generate their own power and cut their energy bills while helping to protect the environment. Unlike utility-scale turbines, small turbines can be suitable for use on properties as small as one acre of land in most areas of the country.

SCIENTISTS HAVE FIGURED OUT HOW TO USE QUANTUM TUNNELING TO HARVEST ELECTRICTY FROM EARTH'S HEAT

Quantum tunnelling can help scientists convert the Earth's surplus infrared radiation and waste heat into electricity.

By India Ashok.

More here: http://www.ibtimes.co.uk/scientists-have-figured-out-how-use-quantum-tunnelling-harvest-electricity-earths-heat-1659802

Feb 8th 2018

Scientists have figured out a way to generate electricity from the Earth's surplus infrared radiation and waste heat, using quantum tunneling. Our planet absorbs massive amounts of sunlight which in turn leads to a near-constant emission of infrared radiation, which is estimated to amount to millions of gigawatts of energy.

Quantum tunneling is a quantum mechanical effect that occurs when a particle moves through a barrier that it ideally should not be able to surmount. For example, in classical physics, a ball rolling up a hill would require a certain amount of energy to get up the hill and to the other side. However, in quantum physics, the ball could dig through the hill with less energy, in effect tunneling through the barrier. Researchers believe this infrared heat "can be harvested 24 hours a day" to generate electricity, using quantum tunneling. The process involves the use of custom- designed antennas that are capable of detecting infrared or waste heat as high-frequency electromagnetic waves, converting these quadrillionth-of-a-second wave signals into electricity.

Since infrared emissions have very small wavelengths and can oscillate thousands of times faster than a typical semiconductor capable of moving electrons, they require nano antennas which can be difficult to create or test. However, according to scientists behind the new study, quantum tunneling can provide the breakthrough required to achieve the goal. "There is no commercial diode in the world that can operate at such high frequency," Atif Shamim, the lead researcher of the new study, from the King Abdullah University of Science and Technology (KAUST) in Saudi Arabia, said in a statement. "That's why we turned to quantum tunneling."

Although some of the previous inventions are currently in their infancy and far from being perfected, eliminating the restrictions the elite impose on anything that isn't in their interest via their tools of control will allow their expeditious development. During that time, we can be educating ourselves, ironing out the details of the creation of our new world, and working on it.

SOLE SOVEREIGNTY

The most important part of this plan is making every single home and human being autonomous. By that I mean that each home will produce its own power, food, biomedicine(s), and whatever else it needs, except the few things that must continue to be mass produced or grown such as grains, materials for textiles (cotton, hemp, etc.), meat, vehicles, etc.. Every one of us will have a comprehensive education, at least an acre of land (possibly/probably two), a vehicle, a home, all the amenities, and an opportunity to contribute to a global collective utilizing their particular skill, if they so desire.

Making everyone self-sufficient removes the possibility that someone can be leveraged or coerced into acting against theirs or their community's best interests, as well as ensuring that no one goes without anything; strong intelligent individuals are the backbone of strong communities and a strong society.

My thought here is utilizing transparent solar cell window panes to create a greenhouse that's a groundfast addition to an existing structure and/or can be incorporated in new structures to generate power for the property as well as be a year-round source of fresh vegetables, herbs, and fruits utilizing the concepts of square-foot and vertical gardening, and composting to maximize efficiency with no environmental footprint other than the space it takes up. In addition to the greenhouse, the existing, or new, structure will also be converted to power generation with solar panel walls, roofs, and windows, as well as compact wind powered dynamos with the vanes incorporated in the roof peak that double as the sensor unit for a full information weather station.

While thinking about the power generation capabilities of our current technologies and reducing our global footprint as much as possible it's impossible not to consider our mobility. Electric vehicles are already a burgeoning market, but they have a distance problem that's currently being addressed by ever-increasing lithium ion battery sizes, which in turn will require higher output chargers and charging stations in the public sphere, adding more infrastructure.

In trying to reduce our footprint it seems counterproductive to me to build additional infrastructure to accommodate electric cars when every single home an electric vehicle passes will be generating power. I suggest utilizing carbon water proton batteries (when perfected) with a couple hundred miles of distance and creating an induction charging system that's incorporated in a gatepost, mailbox post, or stands alone, that wirelessly charges each vehicle as they pass until solar powered vehicles with the hoods, roofs, trunk lids, and windows of the vehicles generating solar power are perfected. Or, we develop a dynamo that charges the vehicle as it moves (a dynamo driven by every rolling wheel could perpetually power every vehicle and may be the answer for the vehicles needed to carry large quantities of freight, like trucks and trains). Every households' fossil fuel powered vehicles should be systematically replaced by electric vehicles as soon as possible.

Everyone in every home must be self-sufficient. Being autonomous versus punching someone else's timeclock will allow us to govern our own lives and live by our circadian rhythms. Working and/or learning to sustain ourselves eight to ten hours a day is enough. No one should have to work at night. That time should be for socializing, entertainment, being with family, doing restful things, or just doing whatever you feel like doing, and of course, sleeping.

If each of us can take care of ourselves completely and are able to provide everything we could possibly need through our acre(s) of land and our immediate community we won't be dependent on anyone and won't need assistance from anyone we don't know. That alone will remove any remaining incentive for crime with money out the equation; there won't be any reason to steal, you'll have all you need, the ability to make more, and a supportive community for assistance if needed.

As for the bulk food items such as grains, nuts, fruits, etc.… Those will be grown communally on common ground in and/or around the community. Each family will figure out how much of each crop they'll consume in a year and be responsible for that portion of the crops' cultivation and processing. Meats will be handled in a similar fashion. Chickens, pigs, and goats can/will be raised and processed on site, with goats doubling as grass and weed abatement, chickens for insect control, and pigs for consumption of whatever isn't composted.

Beef and dairy cattle, and sheep will graze communally in numbers enough to provide each family with all they need and be processed in the community. Hemp will be planted on all unused land until it can be reforested in order to provide renewable biological carbon sinks and material for multiple forms of textiles; with the reforesting taking place on land that will never be used, except for carbon sinks as old infrastructure is removed and recycled. Each community will generate enough food stuffs to create a slight overage that can be forwarded to a global collective if need be that can be used to help other areas catch up or in case of emergencies.

The natural forms of everything now considered "illicit drugs" will be allowed with the stipulation that one must grow and process their own. There will be no transference to other parties for any reason and any adulteration will bring about a severe penalty that will be discussed later in this narrative. For example, if you want to smoke tobacco or marijuana, you'll have to grow and process your own; if you want to smoke opium, you'll have to grow your own poppies and process the sap yourself. Only natural forms of use will be acceptable. Alcoholic beverages will be discouraged but not prohibited unless they become the problem they are now.

Earlier I said I'd elaborate on the societal and governmental system I propose we adopt and this is probably a good place to do it. The Andaman Islanders had a system that A.R. Radcliffe-Brown described as matricentrism. In this system the family was the first form of government. The needs of everyone in the family were looked after equally by the men and women. There was a distinct division of labor with men working away from home, women working close to home, and children learning about both spheres before being sent to learn the work their gender entailed.

The community was the next form of government. It was led by the man who was most popular, had the most even temperament, and the most knowledge and success at everything required to survive. The other men made up a committee that represented every family with the elderly serving as a "voice of reason and experience" and the women having the final say in every decision made, especially conflict, a decision that was governed by them almost exclusively.

I propose we create a community government loosely based on the above description that takes care of the needs of everyone in the community and instead of having the massive corrupt state and federal bureaucracies peopled with stupid, selfish, squabbling, amoral, agenda-driven, do-nothing idiots we have now we utilize the repurposed communication technologies of these now defunct nations/governments to include everyone in all the decision making above the community level.

To do this all we need is a news reader to broadcast whatever proposal or problem the people need to turn their attention to into every home in the affected area, or globally if need be, via the television, with all the information on the subject and all possible outcomes being broadcast as well. Via that same device everyone can select the most favorable outcome and respond. The responses can be tallied algorithmically and the results displayed on the device within a few minutes, hours, or days depending on the size of the population and area affected. If the result is accepted by everyone, we can then proceed to the remediation stage. If not, we can hold another informational round that identifies any discrepancies, any questions, or additional possible outcomes and vote again until a consensus is reached. This system will allow everyone to have a say in the solution and be fully aware of all outcomes. It will also reduce the response and reaction times to days or weeks versus the years, or sometimes never, we now
experience from our self-proclaimed "leaders" that do as much nothing as they possibly can in order to maintain their useless positions of "authority."

The following are some of the most obvious advantages of the form of matricentric agrarian community centered lifeway I propose. Others will manifest as progress is made, as will any possible disadvantages, which will allow us to address them before they become major problems.

- First and foremost, this form of agrarian matricentrism will eliminate the pollution and carbon emission footprint of commercial agriculture and ranching and eliminate the need for power plants, massive solar arrays and wind farms, and all associated infrastructure around the globe which will radically reduce carbon and chemical emissions and free up a lot of green space for biological carbon sinks. It will end all the toxic activities related to fossil fuels, natural gas, hydroelectrics, and nuclearization, the destruction these activities cause, and allow the reclamation of lands dedicated to those activities to commence. The only thing that will have a larger impact on zero carbon and pollution elimination is planting hemp for useable and renewable biological carbon sinks on all reclaimed land until trees can be replanted in areas that will never be used.

- By eliminating power plants and the associated infrastructure we'll also eliminate the inherent blackouts, wildfires, and other systemic problems that come with them as they fail, as well as ending the need to constantly maintain, replace, and add to them, which eliminates their constant expansion and the resulting loss of green space.
- The physical activity of working around one's home and community, gardening, taking care of animals, processing foods and medicinal herbs will reduce stress and increase metabolism, resulting in weight loss and improved fitness, which, in turn, will reduce or eliminate the effects of stress and weight related diseases, i.e. diabetes, insulin resistance, hypertension, high blood pressure, etc. and boost one's immune system efficacy and sense of well-being.
- Poverty, hunger, isolation, ignorance, stupidity, and homelessness will be eliminated.
- Communal activity will allow neighbors to connect and work together developing a real community versus just being a group of people that happen to share proximity without knowing each other. This will exponentially increase positive human contact, which in turn will have a huge positive effect on mental and physical health.
- Eating fresh home-grown food infused with medicinal herbs will drastically reduce exposure to toxins and increase one's overall health exponentially.
- Including fresh gown medicinal herbs specific to one's medical needs as well as for general overall health in one's diet will increase overall health and transition one to preventive healthcare from the current curative system of toxic drugs with multiple adverse side effects.
- Ending the mass spraying of herbicides and pesticides associated with current commercial farming practices will detox the environment and in turn humanity over time, reducing all the adverse effects mentioned in the 'I KILL YOU' section of this

book, increasing individual physical and mental health and well-being.

- Ending the current model of commercial agriculture and ranching will allow us to reclaim/repurpose a large portion of that land and begin reforesting the planet.
- Growing hemp on all the reclaimed lands while we're reforesting them will create a crop with a myriad of uses while doubling as renewable biological carbon sinks that scrub five times the carbon of trees, accelerating the removal of the existing carbon in the atmosphere and shading the earth from the sun's rays, which will cool the planet's surface.
- This form of agrarianism will end the need for a large amount of the plastics related to food packaging and shipping. The remaining packaging needed can be converted to reusable glass for liquids and hemp paper for the wrapping/packaging of solids.
- The local production and consumption of all food stuffs and necessities will end the ridiculous practice of 'commerce', one of the most wasteful and toxic enterprises mankind currently engages in.

For example, years ago I picked up a load of strawberries in Stockton, California and delivered them to Eastern Market in Detroit, Michigan. I then deadheaded to a farm in central Michigan for a load of strawberries that I delivered to Market St. in San Francisco. The fuel wasted and the pollution created by trucking two loads of strawberries almost 5000 miles is ridiculous compared to the amount of fuel not used, or pollution not created, to truck one load the 100 miles to Frisco from Stockton and the other the 100 miles to Eastern Market from the farm, not to mention, the freshness lost. That was just a small example of 'commerce' as we're now shipping containers full of locally grown meat to China for processing and shipping the finished product back here for consumption, which is wrong on too many levels to go into, but I'm sure you've heard about some of them on the news…recalls for foreign objects (plastics, metals, etc.), toxic chemicals, bacterial diseases, etc.…

- Potable water will likely be the most difficult thing to tackle in some places, since ninety percent of the world's water is unusable, aquifers are severely depleted, and infrastructure is toxic and failing in many areas. Therefore, we'll have to upgrade and use existing systems until we find alternatives. Some of you may be thinking collecting rainwater is the answer and I would encourage everyone to do so with this warning…the water should be tested before use (atmospheric pollutants come down with the rain), and it's not a consistent enough water source to depend on in some areas.

- The current sewage and septic systems will also have to be used until better alternatives are found, or improvements on existing systems can be made.

ADOPT PREVENTATIVE BIOMEDICINES

Transitioning from the curative pharmaceutical form of "medicine" to preventive biomedicines is an extremely important integral part of the following portion of the plan to reverse climate change and the devolution of humanity. As you've already read many of the pharmaceuticals used currently are neurotoxins and carcinogens, even those we're told are safe. Biomedicines incorporated in our diets are the only way to counter the epidemic of toxic medicines big pharma is pumping into society.

Every indigenous people has used a plethora of biomedicines to maintain their health for thousands of years while living in conditions much more rigorous than ours. I'm talking about people that live much closer to nature and the elements than we do and are far healthier than the average modern man. Their success is due primarily to their use of medicinal herbs in their diet. The Andaman Islanders use 119 herbs to successfully treat 159 diseases and provide birth/population control. This isn't lost on the pharmaceutical companys' chemists that have been in the Andaman Islands invading the islanders' territories for decades finding and analyzing their herbs, and for all intents and purposes stealing them.

The elite have categorized knowledge of herbal medicines as "intellectual property" and claimed the Andaman Islanders have no "intellect" therefore they can have no intellectual property, nor can they lay any claim to the islands they inhabited for over sixty thousand years because Whites, specifically the British, have inhabited the islands since the 1600's, making them their territory not the islanders'.

The problem with the pharmaceutical companys' take on the herbal medicines is they, and their chemists, think that by extracting what they think is the "active ingredient" in the herbs and putting it in pill form they'll get the same results the islanders get by using the whole herb in poultices, teas, or dietary additions and they couldn't be more wrong.

The active ingredients are usually a toxin used to kill a bacteria, virus, or parasite which are also toxic to the subject. Using just the active ingredient is just as toxic for the user as it is for the malady it's treating and often causes equal harm to both. Nature has a remedy for that in the rest of the plant that the chemists deem useless and discard.

Along with the active ingredient the plant contains enzymes, amino acids, and alkaloids that act as enhancers, buffers, timers, and often direct the active ingredient to the specific area it's needed instead of simply flooding every cell in the body with it. Using them in poultices, teas, and food provides the proper dose to the proper location for the proper amount of time. Adopting the practice in our new paradigm will increase overall health (physical and mental) and eliminate the need for multiple pharmaceutical companies and the bulk, if not all, of their toxic cocktails.

ROUND UP THE HOMELESS

I think we need to begin by empowering the most disenfranchised in our society before anyone else. To that end we need to round up the homeless. There's a large auditorium or arena in every town. A sports arena, or school gymnasium, would be ideal because they would have locker rooms with showers, which would give people a place to get cleaned up and into some new clothes.

As individuals complete that stage they can be triaged, with those needing nothing more than a home being given one, transported there and set up with whatever incidentals they need and for further assistance in the coming days. Those needing more, healthcare, mental healthcare, etc. can be categorized and given the help they need to be successfully homed and reintegrated into society. The next step will be to begin educating them as to what we're doing so they can participate too.

Helping the homeless in other parts of the world will probably be a more complex endeavor due to extreme poverty, undereducation, and homelessness being endemic, generational, and hereditary in some countries, as well as extremely lower levels of overall health and a general lack of available healthcare, but we can't allow that to deter us from putting a roof over everyone's head and bringing them up to speed with the world we're creating. No one gets left behind this time no matter what challenges are encountered and helping those that need it most first will guarantee it doesn't happen.

END ALL CONFLICT

"UNDER PEACEFUL CONDITIONS A WARLIKE MAN SETS UPON HIMSELF." – Friedrich Nietzsche, *Beyond Good and Evil*

"TO SEE OTHERS SUFFER DOES ONE GOOD, TO MAKE OTHERS SUFFER EVEN MORE: THIS IS A HARD SAYING BUT AN ANCIENT, MIGHTY, HUMAN, ALL-TOO-HUMAN PRINCIPLE TO WHICH EVEN THE APES MIGHT SUBSCRIBE: FOR IT IS SAID THAT IN DEVISING BIZARRE CRUELTIES THEY ANTICIPATE MAN AND ARE, AS IT WERE, HIS "PRELUDE."" – Friedrich Nietzsche, *On the Genealogy of Morals*

Archaeological evidence indicates that man has engaged in conflict since before he began walking upright. The longitudinal studies of our nearest primate ancestor, chimpanzees, have shown us that we use tactics very similar to theirs, only more refined, in our conflicts, which indicates our propensity for violence is inherent. The earliest evidence of conflict has been found in the fossils of the earliest iterations of man and evidence of organized conflict has been found in Neanderthal graves, with evidence of conflict by organized armies dating back well over thirteen thousand years. Historical evidence indicates that man has been at war somewhere on the planet since 2700 B.C…That's 4720 years of constant war.

As soon as the elite rose to power out of the ashes of the hunter-gathers they created a culture of conflict by psuedospeciating along the abstract/imaginary lines of culture/race and have continued creating imaginary lines based on wealth or lack thereof, religion or lack thereof, government or lack thereof, and a highly evolved hierarchy of race that categorizes anyone that isn't white as inferior and therefore worthy of annihilation, subjugation, oppression, and enslavement that continues to this day.

The modern world is now at war with everything and the world is burning for all intents and purposes, with the elite fanning the flames in their lust for profit. Everyone is fighting something, if not a myriad of things, and the list grows daily. To say we have a culture of conflict is now one of the greatest understatements ever uttered; we're even fighting conflict now and it's time we end the eternal battles that fill the elite's coffers and our graveyards, erase the imaginary battle lines and cooperate with each other. The survival of humankind depends on it.

"FINAL CONSIDERATION"
"IF WE COULD DISPENSE WITH WARS, SO MUCH THE BETTER. I CAN IMAGINE MORE PROFITABLE USES FOR THE TWELVE BILLION NOW

PAID ANNUALLY FOR THE ARMED PEACE WE HAVE IN EUROPE; THERE ARE OTHER MEANS OF WINNING RESPECT FOR PHYSIOLOGY THAN FIELD HOSPITALS. – GOOD; *VERY* GOOD EVEN: SINCE THE OLD GOD IS ABOLISHED, I AM PREPARED TO *RULE THE WORLD"* – Friedrich Nietzsche, *Nietzsche's drafts*

END OUR PARTICIPATION IN EVERYTHING HARMFUL

Leading by example is the best way to show the rest of the world how to move forward with the shift. That being said, one of the very first things we should do is end all forms of aggression the world over and bring all our people home. That doesn't pertain just to the military, I mean everyone; that especially includes the spooks and ghosts that belong to alphabet agencies that are committing subversive acts and disrupting foreign affairs around the globe, as well as ambassadors, emissaries, and representatives of the current paradigm.

As we're ending the hostilities, we also need to be ending the production and use of everything toxic, no matter what use we're putting them to. We didn't have all this toxic stuff in our environment 100 years ago and the main reason we have it now is because someone became wealthy creating and producing it, not because it was a necessity. In fact, much of what we use today was just one of many things devised to address a past problem, we're using it today because those with the money devised a way to capitalize on it and starved out, bought out, and in some cases murdered everything that could/would be better for us.

For example, when I was a kid, we got a small newsletter called *'The Weekly Reader'* when I was in grade-school. When I was in the fifth grade there was an article about a farmer in Iowa that devised a method of running an internal combustion engine on plain water. The pictures that accompanied the article showed him filling his 63 Chevy Impala, his pickup truck, and his tractor with a hose that ran from the handpump on his well to the fuel tank fills of the vehicles with captions explaining what we were seeing. Along with those photos were several pictures of the system he'd created to convert water to a viable fuel and a highly simplified explanation of how it worked, as well as how easily it adapted to all his vehicles.

His system was hailed as a scientific breakthrough of epic proportions and he was being called a genius on par with Einstein and Edison. The article continued by saying that allegedly all the big automobile manufacturers were beating a path to his door with huge checks in an attempt to buy his design with quotes from several auto makers on how his invention would revolutionize the auto industry and the world in general, making it cleaner and more economical. The mayor of Los Angeles (the most polluted city in the country then) was also quoted as saying that it would be just what California needed to eliminate the horrendous smog problem its cities faced.

I don't remember the exact timeframe. Not long after the initial article a follow-up article in our '*Weekly Reader*' contained a picture of the farmer holding up a check for $200,000 from one of the big three auto makers and shaking hands with a man in a suit, while several other suits looked on smiling. When asked what he was gonna do with the money, the farmer stated that he didn't really know, that farming had been his family's life for generations and that he was gonna continue doing that, mainly because he enjoyed it and he couldn't imagine just sitting around doing nothing.

A few weeks later, on the 'NBC Nightly News with Chet Huntley and David Brinkley' they did a story on the farmer, but it wasn't a happy one. It seems that a stipulation of the purchase of his invention was that he would have to turn over everything he had that pertained to the invention and he wasn't aware of or didn't understand that part. Federal agents had swarmed his property, searched every inch of it, taken all his vehicles, farm equipment, diagrams, notes, parts, and tools that he'd used to design and build his invention, along with IRS agents putting a tax-lien on the property because he hadn't paid the taxes on the $200,000. Again, he didn't know he had to, at least not until he did his taxes at the end of the year. The very last image we saw was him standing in his empty driveway as they hauled away all his farm equipment and vehicles. As you well know Detroit never made any vehicles that ran on water.

Before you cry bullshit and balk at ending corporate toxicity, let me assure you we're not gonna revert to horse and buggy days. The goal here is to restore balance to a drastically imbalanced system that's raping every resource available due to the current "waste more, want more" mentality that's driven by, and driving, today's out of control corporatism while maintaining, and eventually improving, our technological level. The mentality that manufacturing must continually expand no matter what the cost to the environment or humanity as long as the money flows generates roughly 50 million metric tons of e-waste per year with that number rising yearly and e-waste is probably the most toxic form of waste most commonly mentioned. That's only a drop in the bucket of the total amount of waste/pollution generated overall.

My thoughts on curbing this phenomenon and reversing the damage we're doing…

- Stop all mining of rare earth elements.

- Recycle all discarded electronics.
- Reduce the number of manufacturers to one per item (one vehicle manufacturer, one cell phone manufacturer, etc.), instead of having a plethora of competing technology manufacturers that are constantly releasing their latest gimmicks/improvements in attempts to one-up each other and corner markets.
- Combine the best technologies from each current manufacturer and manufacture one make of each unit…phones, appliances, vehicles, etc.
- Manufacture optimized items with an indefinite life-span that can be easily upgraded/updated as new technologies become available.
- Create centrally located production zones on each continent taking the location of raw material sources into consideration, instead of having individual factories scattered all over the landscape polluting numerous places to make one item.
- Create a low to no emissions distribution and storage system that services all areas within the production zones' service areas. My thought is utilizing whatever rail systems we need and removing and recycling the rest. The trains will be electric, possibly utilizing dynamos powered by each wheel as a self-perpetuating source of power. The same for the trucks that move freight from the railheads to the distribution areas and in turn individual "retail" sites.

You can bet corporatists will claim the previous plan will be impossible to accomplish; insist their current globalistic system is the only viable method of production and the plan is "isolationist." I would counter that the corporatists' form of forced trade has always been a source of contention and been the cause of more enmity and conflict than it has amenity and cooperation. Not to mention pollution on a grand scale.

The purpose of the previous points is to end all unnecessary transportation of raw materials and goods. The current system of generating raw materials in one area of the world, shipping them to another area for manufacture, and shipping the finished products around the globe for consumption is one of the major contributors to the emission of a myriad of pollutants, not just the carbon emitted by the manufacturing and shipping methods.

Locating all manufacturing in one production zone will drastically reduce shipping and the pollution it creates, as well as increase the ability to contain and recycle, utilize, or neutralize, all pollutants generated during production. While using the recyclables as materials for production we can develop a zero emissions method to secure new raw materials if ever needed, create synthetic materials, or a method to create the same item using totally different non-polluting processes and/or materials.

NO MORE IMMIGRANTS

We need to end the idea that we're anything but citizens of this planet and as such have the inherent right to live wherever we desire. I would ask those once deemed immigrants by the idiocracy to choose an area of knowledge that will be needed to rebuild their homeland, learn as much about it as possible and gain as much practical experience while helping get the ball rolling, then go home and use your knowledge and experience to help rebuild your homeland. We'll be right beside you. No one will be left behind, unless they want to be, meaning indigenous that wish to continue their lifeway. I would bet anything, given the same high standard of living around the globe, people would much rather be in their cultural home than anywhere else. I know I would if I had a cultural homeland.

MERITOCRACY ABOVE THE BASELINE
IF YOU CONTRIBUTE, YOU'LL BE REWARDED, IF YOU DON'T CONTRIBUTE, YOU'LL STILL BE INCLUDED.

In every society around the globe there will be people that are happy with the baseline and will only want to work enough to maintain it (hopefully not many, I'd like to see every individual live to their fullest potential and help move civilization forward). And, there will always be those that seek to further humanity and push the boundaries of knowledge and ability (this time "should I" will take a front seat to "can I"). Those people should be rewarded for their contributions above and beyond the societal baseline commensurate with their contribution(s), as should those that work to get everyone to the baseline during the transition from dystopia to utopia.

My thoughts on the transition are that we start with the most underserved and marginalized in every society around the globe. That means the most remote individuals in the most remote communities that wish to be involved, giving all indigenous peoples the choice of altering their lifeways to join us in the new paradigm or to remain without encroachment as they are, of course. We begin to transition the existing homes, or build new homes, in our starting points by educating the people affected in how to construct and use their new home and environment effectively as we build them. When their home is done, I would ask that they contribute to the building of their neighbors' homes because their knowledge and experience will be invaluable, especially when encountering new regional, geographical, or locational (rural, suburban, or urban) challenges.

My thoughts here are that we can create a snowball effect of our own increasing the speed and area of our progress as we progress in order to encompass the globe and get everyone on an equal baseline as soon as is humanly possible for the sake of our planet and all its citizens. It won't be easy in the beginning but as we gain experience it will become like second nature. By the time we get to more challenging locations we'll be adept at all the skills required to tackle the toughest jobs with ease.

Personally, I would like to see the beginnings of the new paradigm spread like wildfire so we can move forward to ever increasing levels of health (both mental and physical), knowledge, intelligence, and cooperation as swiftly as possible. As well as renewing the stability of our environment at the same time.

The more one contributes the more one gets for their contributions, up to a point. We can't allow a massive societal disparity to happen again. That's when people get left behind, giving poverty of every sort and its cohorts such as crime an opportunity to rear their ugly heads. My suggestion is that the reward for contributions be a fluid thing with the contributors being rewarded with things of their choice being previously negotiated instead of assigned arbitrarily. It doesn't make sense to me to have a standardized reward system that may not contain the thing someone really wants or needs.

END THE INJUSTICE SYSTEM

"IT IS PRECISELY AMONG CRIMINALS AND CONVICTS THAT THE STING OF CONSCIENCE IS EXTREMELY RARE; PRISONS AND PENITENTIARIES ARE *NOT* THE KIND OF HOTBED IN WHICH THIS SPECIES OF GNAWING WORM IS LIKELY TO FLOURISH: ALL CONSCIENTIOUS OBSERVERS ARE AGREED ON THAT, IN MANY CASES UNWILLINGLY ENOUGH AND CONTRARY TO THEIR OWN INCLINATIONS. GENERALLY SPEAKING, PUNISHMENT MAKES MEN HARD AND COLD; IT CONCENTRATES; IT SHARPENS THE FEELING OF ALIENATION; IT STRENGTHENS THE POWER OF RESISTANCE." – Friedrich Nietzsche, *On the Genealogy of Morals*

The current system of laws and their enforcement created by the wealthy to protect their interests is one of the most corrupt systems ever instituted. Initially, it was used by the elite as a means to secure the slave labor they built their fortunes with prior to and during the industrial revolution. In the last few decades the elite bought the prisons and many of the systems utilized by the county jails and created a for-profit prison system that's grown exponentially thanks mainly to poverty, alphabet agencies flooding the streets with drugs, the gutting of the education system, the elite exporting their manufacturing businesses to China and Mexico with the blessings of bought-off politicians, offshoring other jobs, and the automation of what remained here, all resulting in a devastating loss of employment for the undereducated that performed the unskilled labor that was once the backbone of American industry.

As with the earlier slave labor system of the industrial revolution one can buy their way out of the current system if they have the money to grease the palms of all the mechanisms of the system…high priced attorneys, crooked cops, politicians and bureaucrats, judges, prosecutors, and probation and parole departments. It's the poor that are relegated to over-worked dump-truck public defenders which results in they're being the ones that keep the beds in the prisons full, and in turn the elite's pockets that own them. Several private prison systems have even sued some states for enacting laws that release prisoners early or not arresting and convicting enough people in the courts to keep their beds full, as well as creating contracts that guarantee a state will maintain at least seventy percent of their facilitys' capacities at all times.

IF PRISONS DETERED CRIME THEY'D BE EMPTY.

"A STRANGE THING, OUR PUNISHMENT! IT DOES NOT CLEANSE THE CRIMINAL, IT IS NO ATONEMENT; ON THE CONTRARY, IT POLLUTES WORSE THAN CRIME DOES." – Friedrich Nietzsche, *The Dawn*

GIVE A LITTLE MAN A LITTLE POWER AND HE'LL THINK HE'S A POWERFUL MAN.

Nothing illustrates the previous sentence better than the mentality of the current policing system, or cops, as they've been called since the early days when their badges were made of copper. They were/are the lowest rung on the ladder of corruption we call the judicial system. They call themselves "the thin blue line' between order and mayhem, but in a great number of cases they are the mayhem, as illustrated on May 25th,

2020 by the murder of George Floyd by Derek Chauvin and three other Minneapolis cops over passing an allegedly counterfeit twenty-dollar bill. Or the murder of Louisville E.M.T. Breonna Taylor on March 13th, 2020 by 3 undercover cops serving a "no-knock" warrant in the middle of the night, to the wrong address, for someone already in custody, or any one of hundreds of murders committed against Black Americans in the 64 years I've been on this planet.

George Floyd's murder sparked a global outrage resulting in thirteen days and nights of protests that were initially violent until Terrance Floyd spoke out against it, reason took hold, and rational minds prevailed, which has since been abandoned as violence escalates in many major cities once again, resulting in "The Donald" sending in federal troops, adding to the violence. I'm sure the idiot in chief, The Donald, will take credit for quelling the violence with his "domination" ideology at some point, but nothing could be further from the truth. That narcissistic self-serving idiot threw gasoline on a civil rights fire that's been smoldering and erupting into flaming cities on occasion since before Dr. Martin Luther King attempted unsuccessfully to bring racial peace to this country in the sixties.

Sadly, the people involved in organizing the current protests believe something will change this time, like they have every time a cop murders a person of color and the country erupts into protests, but I'll tell you exactly what will happen…the elite's minions, by minions I mean their politicians and bureaucrats will make a big show of going on national television, talking in circles around pointed questions, making a litany of empty promises like disbanding, or defunding, police departments, and claiming empathy with the protesters.

They'll initiate legislation that bans chokeholds and/or knee-holds and no-knock warrants like they've done so many times before, ban confederate flags and other "symbols of racism," rehash other promises like body and car cams, promise "investigations" into other acts of police violence, allude to other symbolic measures, promise to enact changes and publicize them through their media outlets. Murderers like Derek Chauvin and his three accomplices will be given stiff sentences. The policemen's' union will strike, or threaten to, some cops will quit, other cops will complain, and the sentences will quietly be reduced to a slap on the wrist during an appeal that happens years after the fact in an effort to prevent more Watts, Ferguson, Seattle, Portland, or Minneapolis riots from breaking out. Police chiefs will go on national television claiming they agree that something should be done but the legislation goes too far, putting their "good cops" lives in jeopardy and the bill will stall for debate somewhere in the elaborate process of making it into law.

In the meantime, the protests will eventually deescalate after a lot of property's been destroyed and all the lip-service convinces the protesters they've "done something." They'll stop entirely when people get tired of having their heads caved in by batons, being tased, being shot with rubber bullets, bean bags, and occasionally real bullets. Life will get back to the abnormal mess it's become. Another pandemic, earthquake, hurricane, tornado, flood, or crisis will catch the news cycle's eye and they'll be off and running with it, relegating the riots to an also mentioned status, which will serve to "normalize" them and alienate the people they're trying to influence.

Whatever bills there are will be quietly shelved and if no one says anything, forgotten. If and/or when it's brought up after the next Black American's murder, the politicians involved will look straight into the cameras on the news with sorrowful, possibly even tearful, faces and say they did the best they could but it was so-and-so's fault it didn't pass and they'll try harder next time if you vote for them again and vote so-and-so out in the next election, or there just wasn't any support or funding, or any one of the hundreds of excuses they use for maintaining the status quo.

I can't count the number of times this scenario's played out in my 64 years but I can guarantee you it'll play out again and again because it's what the elite want to happen, otherwise racial inequality and the ensuing police violence would've never taken place and Martin Luther King would still be with us.

Comprehensive education for every single person, a total paradigm shift resulting in a balanced environment and society, and the end of the rule of money and those who possess it is the only way to end the rampant disparity and create equality across the board, which is the only solution to this society's current plague of problems.

Eighteen days after the fact, the measures I mentioned previously are beginning to happen around the country, including some additional measures. Reallocating police funding toward social services and education is being discussed, statues of icons linked to racial issues are being destroyed, renaming military bases named for confederate soldiers is being considered, and Trump is opposing all of it, claiming he will use the military to enforce his decisions if he feels it's necessary. This ensures a protracted fight will go on well into next year between the Trump administration and those calling for change, or at least until Joe Biden's inaugurated if he wins the election, which is entirely possible because Trump is doing his best to alienate the minority vote, and many others, with his rhetoric and actions.

Three months after the fact, social destruction, rioting, looting, property destruction, shootings, armed encounters with city, state, and federal forces, and the burning of governmental properties are still going on under the guises of civil rights protests ensuring that whatever measures were promised will never be enacted. In fact, the exact opposite will end up happening, as is usually the case.

As of September 9th, 2020 protests are going on in 2400 cities, violently in 220 of them and spreading.

AN ARMED SOCIETY IS A POLITE SOCIETY
A SHOOTER CAN ONLY SUCCEED IF THEY HAVE UNARMED VICTIMS.

CRIMINALS LOVE UNARMED VICTIMS.

WHEN GUNS ARE OUTLAWED ONLY OUTLAWS WILL HAVE GUNS.

Although it would be the epitome of insanity to arm the public in its current state, as evidenced by the rising tide of gun violence. Nonetheless, once educated everyone should be armed. Every newborn should be issued a weapon at birth and education in its use and care should be an integral part of their enculturation with ultimate proficiency as the end goal.

To those thoroughly indoctrinated in the current 'learned helplessness' system and the 'it's the government's responsibility to protect me' propaganda I'm sure this is frightening just to read, but let me ask you this…would you prefer to have the knowledge, power, and right/duty to protect yourself and your property or would you rather leave your well-being in the hands of others that arrive after the fact and more often than not only make a report about your death or loss, or, as is becoming the norm, kill you as they "mistake" you for a perpetrator during their ensuing adrenaline rush? It's a highly skewed world we live in where you have no right to protect your property, criminals have more rights than their victims, and those tasked with protecting you kill you instead. Protecting your property and yourself is the only reasonable alternative.

I'm sure opponents of an armed populace will scream that it will be absolute mayhem with gunfights breaking out constantly and bullets flying everywhere all day and night and it absolutely would, given the current state of inhumanity. Gun opponents claim there's plenty of history to support that claim, but it should be pointed out that gunfights weren't nearly as plentiful as Hollywood would have you believe, it was confined primarily to frontier areas, lasted only about twenty years, and it was during a time when the intelligence of the average gun-toting individual was far lower than it is now, or will be once everyone's educated.

With education, increased intelligence, and high levels of prosperity for all will come a radical decrease in crime, if not the end, and a new perspective on personal responsibility. Additionally, the knowledge that you can be killed as easily as you can kill will temper whatever kill-craziness that opponents claim will ensue. Granted, there's a high probability that initially a few people will try their newfound freedom irresponsibly and that will have to be dealt with accordingly when The Law is broken, but it won't last long when the population sees the outcome.

ONE LAW, ONE PENALTY

Libraries are filled with books on jurisprudence (law), which is a good indication of how complex and corrupt the existing legal system is. So corrupt in fact, that it often looks like criminals benefit more than their victims in many instances, especially when they're rich. Personally, I consider any judicial system that doesn't allow one to unequivocally protect one's property in its entirety extremely corrupt. Not to mention, this system's ability to be swayed by the monieds' wealth, power, social status, and political connections.

As previously stated, when taken as a whole the current judicial system in this country is just a staging ground for the filling of the elite's for-profit prisons with the poorest, most undereducated, and underserved in the country, mainly because they're the easiest to victimize from birth to death and because it's easy to sway an ignorant public's opinion against them.

That said, I think it the epitome of unfair that we change the world without changing what we constitute as crime by extremely simplifying the legal code to accommodate the highly intelligent world we will be creating, as a comprehensive education for all will be an integral part of ending the degradation of the planet and the accompanying devolution of society.

It's been my experience that with education and increased intelligence comes temperance. I would posit that once homed in an autonomous setting with the same advantages as everyone around them ninety-nine point nine percent of the current prison population would be just as responsible as anyone that hasn't been incarcerated, quite possibly even more so because they've experienced the difference between right and wrong personally and have no illusions that everything they do is right.

As we've leveled the societal playing field so should we level the legal playing field with one simple immutable law, 'harm no one or nothing' and one penalty, death, for breaking that law (littering is harmful). Under this new system everyone currently incarcerated should get a chance for a new life as well.

To that end I would release all non-violent offenders immediately and get them homed so they can be brought up to speed on the new paradigm we're creating. As for the violent offenders…they should be interviewed, given psychological evaluations, and all evidence in their cases should be reviewed completely to eliminate every crack that someone could slip through with the acquitted released and those deemed rabidly unrepentant or unredeemable executed. I'm relatively sure that alone will give anyone questioning the one law, or thinking they're above it, for whatever reason, pause.

INSTITUTE THE PERSONAL JUSTICE SYSTEM

As I previously stated people should have the right to protect their property in its entirety as well as their lives and the lives of their family members if need be. It doesn't make much sense to simplify the law and maintain a complex enforcement system of cops, courts, jails, and prisons, especially in the midst of an educated, responsible, fully armed populace that exists on an even footing. Therefore, we should simplify the justice system as well and nothing can be fairer than justice being meted out immediately at the scene of the crime by the wronged, their agents, or in the case of an environmental crime the environment's agent. In fact, it should be everyone's duty to enforce The Law whenever they witness a transgression.

Before you go losing your mind and screaming it'll be vigilante chaos in the streets, think about this…we're talking about educated intelligent people now that will only require one example to make an impression on them, if that. Not only that, it's highly unlikely that given a population of highly intelligent people with common goals and no disparity there'll even be any crime.

END BREAD AND CIRCUS
Sports, the opiate of the masses.

IF PEOPLE CARED ABOUT THE ENVIRONMENT HALF AS MUCH AS
THEY CARED ABOUT A MEANINGLESS SPORTS FIGURE, TEAM, OR
EVENT, THE WORLD WOULDN'T BE IN THIS MESS.

The social manipulation tactic of "Bread and Circus" was created and perfected by the Romans and used as the ultimate social distraction by the emperors in order to conceal theirs and the senate's corruption from the people. By mesmerizing the ignorant masses with a spectacular blood bath of carnage and bombarding them with loaves of bread and trinkets during their "games" in The Coliseum and other arenas throughout the empire they placated the citizenry into mindless unquestioning ignorance and obedience. Modern sports are just the refined continuation of bread and circus, which is now pumped into every home since the advent of the television and every hand via the internet and smartphones.

Without the incentive of multi-million-dollar payouts I doubt very much that sports figures will want to continue going out and injuring themselves just for the love of the game(s). That aside, for the moment at least, all distractions need to be reduced as much as possible so people can concentrate on the tasks at hand, especially those that must be educated in order to bring them up to speed on the new paradigm, which I'm going to guess would be a vast majority of sports figures too, mainly because for quite a while now sports has been the surrogate for education in relation to making a good living. Once everyone's on a level playing field and cooperating, we can revisit organized sports, if that's what's desired. Until then the mediums used to broadcast sports events are better used educating everyone.

END CURRENT DAYTIME PROGRAMMING

Currently a vast majority of what's considered "entertainment" is mainly mindless drivel with little to no socially redeeming value, often designed as nothing more than a distraction. Most of the "news" is designed to steer its watchers toward one agenda or another. In fact, almost everything on television is designed to normalize what was once considered abnormal and support the elite's agendas and paradigm, either passively or actively. As with everything man creates that could be used to further his intelligence it's being used to keep people ignorant, stupid, distracted, and propagandized into being loyal to harmful ideologies and actions.

REPURPOSE EXISTING TECHNOLOGY

Governments have always had the upper hand in the technological race. It's been claimed by the elite that without conflict to drive societies forward technologically in a continued effort to gain a strategic upper hand in the venues of communication, surveillance, mobilization, and weaponization they would simply stagnate at whatever point that competition stopped.

To that end every major government in the world, especially the United States, Russia, and China have a myriad of the latest and greatest technological advancements in the works and operating currently that the general population knows nothing about. Those much more in the know than I claim governments are 10 to 30 years more technologically advanced than the general public. I for one would like to know how true that is, wouldn't you? I'll go one step further by saying that if that's so, those technologies should be repurposed for the advantage of educating societies, not to spy on them and proliferate conflict, but to connect them and enhance our ability to communicate and cooperate more easily.

CREATE A GLOBAL COMMUNICATION NETWORK

In my estimation education and communication are the two most important keys to creating a balanced environment and peaceful society. If we created a global communication network that serviced every single abode on the planet it would go a long way towards shrinking the number of dividing lines the elite have created by keeping us apart and ignorant of each other. They would no longer be able to promote their pseudospeciation agenda in a void of ignorance and push their propaganda into that void to keep us suspicious and hateful.

It would also be a great tool in the elimination of the elite's corrupt, squabbling, do-nothing governments when used as I outlined earlier in other sections of this work. Instead of just believing you have a voice because you've been conditioned to and manipulated into voting for the selection of idiots the elite provided, using the repurposed technologies as I advocate you can and will have a voice in every single thing that goes on in the world.

UTILIZE THE NETWORK FOR EDUCATIONAL PURPOSES
"WHOEVER LEARNS MUCH UNLEARNS ALL VIOLENT DESIRE." –
Freidrich Nietzsche, *Thus Spoke Zarathustra*

"VIOLENCE BEGINS WHERE KNOWLEDGE ENDS." – Abraham Lincoln

INTELLIGENCE CAN'T BE LEGISLATED. EDUCATION IS THE ONLY ANSWER TO IGNORANCE.

People are under the radical misconception that what schools are currently providing is "education" but it's really just indoctrination into the system of debt-slavery. Being taught to do a job, get to that job, and provide the proper emotional kneejerk reaction to the propaganda pumped out by the media isn't education and it's certainly not knowledge, it's a very insidious form of societal manipulation that propagates the agenda of the wealthiest while creating a society of unknowing debt-slaves.

The Humanities is the most important education needed, which is why it's the least promoted. If the people knew the truth of our origins, how this social structure was built, by whom, and for what reason I doubt very much it would exist. The very first lie that needs to be dispelled is that of "discovery."

One can't "discover" anything, or anywhere, that's already populated by a people. The truth is, white Europeans marched around the world with their imaginary sky-god, fake religions, all-consuming greed, and ignorant highly propagandized armies invading areas already populated by long established societies and consumed them, exterminating the vast majority of their people with diseases and violence, stealing everything they considered valuable, sending it back to their incredibly greedy elite, and enslaving those that survived in a myriad of ways.

They descended like a plague on the unknowing indigenous convincing their rulers that their imaginary sky-god was better with trinkets, trickery, and the lies of heaven, hell, salvation, and the "better life" of what they considered "civilization." They destroyed every civilization they encountered by forcing their European lifeways on them irregardless of the harm they inflicted. Then rewrote history to make themselves appear to be benevolent "discoverers" that brought "civilization" to an uncivilized world with their oppression, genocide, unfettered greed, and the pollution of commercial agriculture and industrialization. This is only one of the multitude of lies you're told by the elite. Next, I'd like to touch on one of the lies that bothers me the most, slavery, which has existed as long as mankind.

The elite's historians would have you believe the Civil War was fought exclusively to end chattel slavery in the south. I covered this thoroughly in ITP so I'm just gonna hit the high points here. The truth is the Civil War was instigated by the northern industrialists that wanted the south's cotton for next to nothing and would stop at nothing to get it.

The same industrialists that used multiple forms of slavery to people their factories and build their infrastructures. They enlisted the aid of a Vermont Congressman and fellow industrialist, Justin S. Morrill, to create and institute a tariff that would cripple the south's ability to continue its trade with the European aristocracy, the purchasers of the south's cotton.

The Morrill Tariff was rammed through congress after all the secessionist congressmen from the southern states had quit congress in protest of the northern industrialist's unsuccessful attempts to pressure James Buchanan into forcing the south to sell its cotton to them for pennies on the dollar. When the tariff passed, the Confederate States of America formed in earnest in an effort to escape the tax, maintain their lifeway, and continue their trade with Europe unfettered. Undaunted, Morrill and his ilk threatened to use the government to enforce the tariff militarily and take the cotton if need be. The Confederacy answered with an army of its own and went to war with the Union Army, whipping them at every turn.

Initially, the "ending of slavery" propaganda was the north's first attempt to coerce people into joining the army and the introduction of that idea to the population at large, but slavery was something they lived with every day in the industrialized north (one never knew when they'd be snatched off the street or "slipped a mickey" in a bar and wake up chained to a machine in a rich man's factory) and they had no desire to fight "the rich man's war."

The Union Army was all but defeated before the first military draft was instituted with an income tax to support the army in 1863, which in a way proves it was a "rich man's war" because if a draftee had $300 he could buy his way out of having to serve. This resulted in the poor being snatched up unceremoniously and forced to fight and a large portion of Irish immigrants straight off the boats being conscripted directly into the army as soon as their feet touched American soil.

The "ending of slavery" propaganda was continued by suffragists and abolitionists (that wanted to abolish all slavery, not just chattel slavery) despite its ineffectiveness as an enlistment tool; it went a long way towards the election of the abolitionist president, Abraham Lincoln, who created the 13th Amendment, which allegedly ended slavery, or did it? The "Black Code" and Jim Crow Laws kept Black Americans actively oppressed and enslaved well until the 1960's.

Slavery is alive and well today. It's simply gone deeper underground and is more insidious, now having a financial base versus a physical one, and is all inclusive. If you're poor you get nothing but piddling government handouts and are relegated to the worst living conditions society has to offer no matter what your skin color, although it's predominantly Blacks that suffer this indignity. There are check cashing and quick cash lending establishments to enslave the poor with astronomical interest rates that ensure they'll be paying off a miniscule loan for the rest of their lives. All they've gotta have is an income to participate in that screwing.

If you're more financially well off you're much less likely to live in the impoverished inner cities and dilapidated urban areas, but you're far from "free" in this debt-based society the elite have created. They've manipulated the financial system to ensure you're saddled with debt as soon as, if not before, you enter the workplace and are penalized with a low credit rating whenever you manage to unburden yourself of it, which limits your purchasing ability commensurate with your lack of debt by precluding you from many large debt-based purchases such as cars and homes, unless you've managed to accumulate a large amount of equity in real property that can be used as collateral. Even then you're still subject to high interest rates.

The only way to maintain a high credit score is by walking a tightrope of debt and payment. The reward for maintaining a high credit score is having the ability to make large purchases with a signature, and a low interest rate. The downside is the possibility of losing everything if your finances go south due to the loss of a job, a divorce, the death of a spouse, anything that limits, or ends, your ability to continue walking the tightrope. With the very least penalty being an exorbitant interest rate (up to a massive twenty-four percent), which negatively affects one's ability to rent a home and get a decent job, as well as access to healthcare and other necessities.

In essence, the only difference between chattel slavery and debt slavery is instead of wearing the chains on your wrists and ankles you sleep comfortably in them, drive them around, and carry them in your pockets and wallet. It's an equal opportunity system, anyone can participate. In fact, the more the merrier in the elite's eyes.

The title of this section pertains to using the global network we create to educate everyone and to that end this is what I propose. Since all IoT devices have two way capabilities and we have the network in place to utilize that capability I suggest we use it to educate everyone in the truth of things and dispel all the myths and lies used to keep us ignorant, stupid, and subservient to the elite's system. By everyone I mean every single person on the planet, with adults mixing work with learning throughout the day at home on IoT devices while kids learn in schools and at home.

One of the most important things I learned during my trip through academia is the more one learns the more one realizes they don't know. Like so many, I once believed the "what I don't know can't hurt me" axiom, "thinking" I knew enough to get by and that was all I needed. That mentality is what brought society to this juncture (what you don't know will destroy everything). There's no better evidence to support this hypothesis than the current level of communicative intelligence displayed by a vast majority of the "journalists" on television and in print.

If the trend is to talk down to the declining intelligence of society, they're doing a great job. For the most part they speak and write like 3rd or 4th grade dropouts. Their commentaries run the gamut of written and spoken ignorance with grammatical, contextual, spelling, and pronunciation errors in great abundance and a stunning lack of knowledge about even the simplest things.

Sure, they can recite the lyrics of the new Beyoncé song because her communicative ability is commensurate with a 4th grader's too…a gross inability to pronounce even simple words correctly and even less ability to spell or use them correctly in the formation of a coherent sentence. I find that rather disturbing in people who have chosen a profession that's entirely dependent on good communication skills. It's no wonder ignorance and stupidity have been normalized, and idolized, how can one learn anything when they don't understand, or misinterpret, what they're reading or hearing?

As destructive as China's release of the Covid-19 virus has been, and will be, it's also served to further the technologies I suggest using in this narrative. I used distance/remote learning very successfully during the first three years of my foray into academia. It's been used much more extensively for all levels of education since the stay-at-home orders were issued in March, which means we have a head start on its perfection and use for the purposes I propose here.

Given a little time, very engaging and educational documentaries on the subjects we need to learn can be created and aired. I know this because I watch quite a bit of PBS programming, which is essentially the type of programming I have in mind as I'm writing this. By simply expanding PBS's system to provide a channel for each subject, an individual could learn much of what's needed very quickly once their language and comprehension skills are brought up to speed.

With thousands of networks and channels available now, I think it would be quite an enjoyable experience to have a channel dedicated to each subject that affects our lives and a channel that applies that knowledge to every individual culture in the world. Learning about and becoming familiar with one's neighbors, especially if they're on the other side of the planet, is the best way to end pseudospeciation and bring the global population together in a collective of understanding and cooperation. Additionally, via IoT it will be entirely possible to communicate directly with anyone else on the planet one desires, which will serve to further increase understanding and the ability to become a truly global community.

The following articles are provided to illustrate how even the remotest areas can be connected and that there's now no excuse for leaving anyone behind in the quest to educate and save the planet and its citizens. Combining these technologies with the repurposed military tech will bring about a global communication system that will empower humanity on an unprecedented level.

ALPHABET'S X WILL USE LIGHT BEAMS TO BRING THE INTERNET TO MILLIONS OF RURAL INDIAN HOUSEHOLDS

By Shushma U. N.

The full story: https://qz.com/1157941/google-x-will-use-light-beams-to-bring-the-internet-to-12-million-households-in-indias-andhra-pradesh-state/

December 15th, 2017

The "moonshot factory" of Alphabet, the tech giant that owns Google, is bringing a wireless internet technology it tested in the stratosphere to connect rural areas in India's Andhra Pradesh state. X, as the company is known, is using Free Space Optical Communications (FSOC) to connect far-flung regions of the state. It involves using beams of light to deliver high-speed, high-capacity connectivity over long distances. X has set up some 2,000 FSOC links in partnership with Andhra Pradesh's telecom company, AP State FiberNet, as part of the state's plan to bring broadband connectivity to 12 million households and thousands of government offices and private enterprises.

SPACEX GIVEN GO-AHEAD FOR BROADBAND SATELLITE SERVICES PLAN

By James Ayre.

The full story: https://cleantechnica.com/2018/03/31/spacex-given-go-ahead-for-broadband-satellite-services-plan/

Mar 31st, 2018

SpaceX has now been given formal approval by the US Federal Communications Commission (FCC) to develop its previously revealed global broadband satellite network, the government agency has revealed. As revealed in a public statement on the matter: "This is the first approval of a US-licensed satellite constellation to provide broadband services using a new generation of low-Earth orbit satellite technologies."

What does this have to do with cleantech you ask? Well, the broadband satellite plans clearly represent a notable part of SpaceX and Tesla CEO Elon Musk's broader plans for both firms. As has been noted by many industry observers (and a fair number of commentators here), it seems fairly likely that SpaceX and Tesla will end up merging in some capacity or other at some point. The reality today is that the firms share some services where synergies are possible — though, there's clearly room for more integration in that regard.

For instance, a SpaceX held satellite communications network would of course allow Tesla to cut or eliminate its reliance upon traditional carriers — with all new Tesla vehicles instead possibly getting their internet services via satellite, as an example. A lot of other possibilities exist as well.

Reuters provides more: "The system proposed by privately held SpaceX, as Space Exploration Holdings is known, will use 4,425 satellites, the FCC said. ... The Federal Aviation Administration said on Wednesday that SpaceX plans to launch a Falcon 9 rocket on April 2 at Cape Canaveral, Florida. 'The rocket will carry a communications satellite,' the FAA said."

"The FCC said SpaceX has been granted authority to use frequencies in the Ka (20/30 GHz) and Ku (11/14 GHz) bands. Musk, who is also the founder and chief executive of electric automaker Tesla Inc, said in 2015 that SpaceX planned to launch a satellite-internet business that would help fund a future city on Mars."

"SpaceX wanted to create a 'global communications system' that Musk compared to 'rebuilding the internet in space.' It would be faster than traditional internet connections, he said.

Those certainly represent grand plans which may or may not come to fruition, but some degree of communications independence does seem likely for both SpaceX and Tesla within the not too distant future.

Update – a portion of the satellites have been launched and are moving into place as I write.

END THE SOCIAL MEDIA SURVEILLENCE STATE

IF SOMETHING'S FREE, YOU'RE THE PRODUCT.

Though the owners of social media claim it was created to unite people by giving them a way to connect with each other. It's actually just the easiest way to surveil a massive portion of the population and create the largest data mining project ever imagined. The surveillance was never necessary. As soon as social media came online people began publicly announcing every stupid action and thought they had. While others began deriding them and announcing their own brand of stupidity.

Very quickly it became the venue(s) to show the entire world how abjectly idiotic and self-absorbed one could be and a competition for the most likes, shares, and thumbs ups ensued that's done nothing but escalate into a global competition for attention and its accompanying cheers and derision. The cheers prompted ever increasing stupidity and the derision prompted depression, isolation, murder, and suicide.

While all that was going on, social media sites gathered every byte of information posted on their sites and every byte of information found anywhere/everywhere about its users; compiling it into personal profiles that were/are sold to the highest bidders for a myriad of nefarious reasons. Turning every user into the commodity of a multi-billion-dollar industry built on the invasion of privacy.

DISMANTLE UNNECESSARY CITIES

The following articles are meant to highlight the availability of technologies capable of turning every energy sink/city into a standalone entity capable of self-sustainability without the necessity of massive solar and wind farms outside their limits that are a blight on the land and require massive amounts of green space to construct, as well as a massive amount of transmission and storage infrastructure that adds to the blight and unnecessary land use.

TESLA TO CONSTRUCT VIRTUAL SOLAR POWER PLANT USING 50,000 HOMES IN SOUTH AUSTRALIA

By Steve Hanley.

https://cleantechnica.com/2018/02/04/tesla-construct-virtual-solar-power-plant-using-50000-homes-south-australia/

Feb 4th, 2018

When Elon Musk offered to build what would be the largest grid storage battery installation in the world in South Australia last year, he set off a chain of events that may have implications for the entire world. In a show of typical Muskian over-the-top bravado, Elon promised to build the entire facility in 100 days or it would be free. It was completed nearly 40 days early. Since then, the project has performed precisely as *advertised, bringing stability to the grid in South Australia and making money for Neoen, the system operator, which recently pocketed $800,000 in 48 hours by absorbing excess electricity from the grid and selling it back to the grid operator later when demand increased.*

Australia — with its abundant sunshine — has already been a leader in rooftop solar, but the country also has blinders on when it comes to power because it sits on vast reserves of coal — enough to meet all the world's energy needs for 1,000 years some people claim. A substantial part of Australia's economy is tied to mining coal and shipping it to India, China, and other Asian countries. That means that, just like in America, coal plays an important role in national politics. As just one example, the grid storage plan in South Australia raised the hackles of quite a few politicians who owe their exalted positions to the generosity of coal companies.

But Musk and his audacity have caused the scales to fall from the eyes of more people Down Under. Now, Tesla and the government of South Australia have announced a stunning new project that could change how electricity is generated not only in Australia but in every country in the world. They plan to install rooftop solar system on 50,000 homes in the next 4 years and link them together with grid storage facilities to create the largest virtual solar power plant in history. And here's the kicker: The rooftop solar systems will be free.

The cost of the project will be recouped over time by selling the electricity generated to those who consume it. "We will use people's homes as a way to generate energy for the South Australian grid, with participating households benefiting with significant savings in their energy bills," says South Australia's premier Jay Weatherill. "More renewable energy means cheaper power for all South Australians."

ELON MUSK'S TESLA PLANS TO GIVE THOUSANDS OF HOMES BATTERIES: HERE'S HOW IT WOULD WORK

By political reporter Nick Harmsen.

More at: http://www.abc.net.au/news/2018-02-04/how-tesla-sa-labor-free-battery-scheme-would-work/9394728

Feb 4th, 2018

South Australia's Labor Premier Jay Weatherill has unveiled what he expects to be a vote-winning power policy before the March state election — 'free' solar panels and Tesla batteries for 50,000 homes. And it's all thanks to the guy on the right. Yep, it's the latest gift in the ongoing bromance between Mr. Weatherill and billionaire Tesla boss Elon Musk, after the pair teamed up to help fund the world's biggest lithium-ion battery (which is already producing power in the South Australian grid).

"Free?" I hear you ask. They say nothing is certain but death and taxes. This deal will involve some of the latter (a $2 million taxpayer-funded grant and $30 million loan to Tesla), plus a significant catch — the power generated by the solar panels and the batteries will not be owned directly by the households but may well be sold back to them via a retailer.

First things first. What is a 'Virtual Power Plant'? A VPP is trendy terminology for distributed electricity generation. It's a bit like the internet. Or bitcoin. The idea is that by sharing surplus energy produced by rooftop solar panels when not being used, all consumers can benefit. Key to these systems are smart meters and other clever technology which can figure out automatically which system is producing surplus power and whether that can be stored or moved to another customer.
The South Australian scheme will see the homes of each participant installed with a 5kw solar system paired with a 5kw/15kwh Tesla Powerwall 2 battery.

As the global population adopts the agrarian lifeway I propose, cities will become increasingly obsolete. There will be no need for the huge skyscrapers that house the offices of the elite's systems' machinations or the people that operate them. Most of the support mechanisms that supply them and their populations will cease to exist but I'm sure there will be enough people clinging to them out of fear of the unknown, or a multitude of other reasons, that we'll need to adapt the new energy and sustenance systems we're using to accommodate them.

To that end I suggest we use as many of the newer glass walled skyscrapers as necessary as "power towers" by converting all the glass windows to solar cells with a wind powered dynamo on the roof and a building next door as a "battery pack" utilizing the proton battery technology. That would eliminate the need of creating a solar/wind farm outside the city and the additional storage and transmission infrastructure to get the power from the farm to the city.

The technologies in the previous articles will be the foundation for that adaptation, with whatever portions of the cities not being used or populated being dismantled and recycled to make room for more biological carbon sinks and gardens for its source of food. I honestly hope all cities will be totally abandoned as time passes and the scars they leave in their passing will one day be all but invisible, but that will be up to the citizens that occupy them.

CREATE AN ENDURING LEGACY

The following articles are presented in toto in an effort to illustrate that there are technologies being created to clean up just about every ecological disaster we've created with our insane quest to suck every petrochemical out of the ground and poison the environment with it in as many ways as humanly possible.

THERE IS AN AREA OF PLASTIC IN THE OCEAN THAT'S THREE TIMES THE SIZE OF FRANCE. THIS 23-YEAR-OLD THINKS HE CAN CLEAN IT UP

By Jackie Flynn Mogensen.

https://www.motherjones.com/environment/2018/04/there-is-an-area-of-plastic-in-the-ocean-I-three-times-the-size-of-france-this-23-year-old-thinks-he-can-clean-it-up/

April 20th, 2018

On Wednesday, among the industrial warehouses and abandoned buildings on Alameda Island, just south of Oakland, California, a small team of engineers began the early stages of constructing "System 001." Its bland name obscures the fact that System 001 is actually a first-of-its-kind, 2,000-foot long device intended to rid the ocean of its trillions of pieces of plastic. This week, the system took one baby step toward finally being ocean-ready.

It's designed sort of like an enormous and porous shower curtain: One long, U-shaped black polyethylene tube will attach to a nylon screen hanging underwater, while the entire device drifts across the ocean, using currents to collect plastic before the debris is ultimately removed. In its final form, the floating plastic-eater will be autonomous and powered by solar energy, meaning it will be controlled by algorithms and free to roam within the ocean's plastic hotspots. And, its curtain-like design prevents marine animals from getting trapped, as they would in a net.

It will be the longest ocean structure ever to be deployed, and the Dutch non-profit behind it, the Ocean Cleanup, hopes a swarm of these U-shaped tubes will remove half of the 1.6-million-square-kilometer Great Pacific Garbage Patch (consisting largely of plastics) floating between California and Hawaii in just five years—and 90 percent of accumulated ocean plastic by 2040.

The effort cannot come soon enough; just last month, a study from the group, published in Nature's Scientific Reports, found that the patch is 16 times larger than previous estimates. On Wednesday, the boyish Ocean Cleanup CEO Boyan Slat said, "It's the first time anyone is doing anything like this. So, it's still very much a beta system...I'm sure there will still be things that will go wrong, but that's why we're doing it, really, to improve it—so eventually we can deploy an entire fleet of these systems."

Despite its size and multi-million-dollar price tag, the project has humble origins. Slat was just 16 years old when a diving trip in Greece inspired him to clean the world's oceans. "I saw more plastic bags than fish," he has said about the trip. He went on to eventually present his idea for a massive, plastic-collecting system in a TEDx talk in 2012, recruited a team in 2013, and in 2014, he and his team raised over $2 million in 100 days to fund the project.

Four years and about $40 million in fundraising later, the 23-year-old Slat is finally seeing his vision come to life. "We're ready to launch the world's first ocean cleanup system," he said Wednesday, standing in front of a blueprint of the contraption. "Which is being built right here." From Alameda, System 001 will be towed along the coast of California and then sent 240 nautical miles offshore, for a "dress rehearsal," of sorts. The team will ensure the system functions properly and look for any damage to the structure caused by towing or rough ocean conditions before deploying it to the Great Pacific Garbage Patch. In the end, if all goes well, 60 of these things will be floating around the Pacific.

Cleaning the world's oceans is no small task. The Great Pacific Garbage Patch alone is three times the size of France. And although the mass production of plastics began about six decades ago, according to the UN, the world now produces hundreds of millions of metric tons of plastic each year—with more than 8 million metric tons of it ending up in the ocean. By 2050, some scientists estimate the seas will hold more plastic than fish.

That's at least part of the reason why the project has seen its fair share of criticism. Roland Geyer, a professor of industrial ecology and green supply chain management at UC-Santa Barbara, tells Mother Jones an effort to clean the Great Pacific Garbage Patch is "somewhat pointless" because the vast majority of plastic in the ocean isn't floating on the surface, and even as you work to clean it up, more plastic enters the ocean every day. "Their heart is in the right place," he says about the Ocean Cleanup. "But I think their efforts could be better off elsewhere."

Despite the criticism, the group has continued raising funds and has shown no sign of altering course. If all preliminary tests go as planned, the team expects to launch their system inside the Great Pacific Garbage Patch, 1,200 nautical miles offshore, this summer, with hopes to bring the first haul of plastic in by the end of the year. The plastics can then be turned into and sold as products, like the Ocean Cleanup sunglasses pictured below.

"Plastic doesn't have to be ocean plastic pollution." Says Slat. "I think it's really time to go clean it up."

MATS MADE OF ACTIVE PROTEINS SOAK UP POLLUTION

Posted by Brett Israel-Berkeley.

This article's in toto: https://www.futurity.org/proteins-mats-pollution-1706742/

Mar 19th, 2018

Scientists have figured out a way to keep certain proteins active outside the cell, which could lead to materials with functions usually only found in living systems. The researchers used the technology to create mats that can soak up and trap chemical pollution.

Despite years of effort to stabilize proteins outside of their native environments, scientists have made limited progress in combining proteins with synthetic components like fibers without compromising protein activity.

The new study, which appears in the journal Science, shows a path toward exploiting the power of proteins outside the cell by demonstrating a way to keep proteins active in synthetic environments. The materials in the study could enable on-demand biochemical reactions, such as in war zones or contaminated sites, where they were once not feasible.

The problem with proteins

"We think we've cracked the code for interfacing natural and synthetic systems," says author Ting Xu, a professor in the materials science and engineering and chemistry departments at the University of California, Berkeley, whose lab led the work. The problem with proteins is that they're finicky. Remove them from their native environments and they will likely fall apart. To function properly, proteins must fold into a specific structure, often with the help of other proteins.

To overcome this challenge, Xu's lab analyzed trends in protein sequences and surfaces to see if they could develop a synthetic polymer that provides all the things that a protein would need to keep its structure and function. "Proteins have very well-defined statistical pattern, so if you can mimic that pattern, then you can marry the synthetic and natural systems, which allows us to make these materials," says first author Brian Panganiban, a former graduate student in Xu's lab who is now a chemist at PolyDrop, a Seattle-based chemical company.

The researchers then created random heteropolymers, which they call RHPs. RHPs are composed of four types of monomer subunits, each with chemical properties designed to interact with chemical patches on the surface of proteins of interest. The monomers are connected to mimic a natural protein to maximize the flexibility of their interactions with protein surfaces. Researchers at Northwestern University ran extensive molecular simulations to show that the RHP would interact favorably with protein surfaces, leading to correct protein folding and stability outside of the cell.

Making materials from proteins

The researchers then tested whether they can use an RHP to create protein-based materials for bioremediation of toxic chemicals. The researchers mixed RHP with a protein called organophosphorus hydrolase (OPH), which degrades the toxic organophosphates found in insecticides and chemical warfare agents.

A GIANT HARPOON CAN DRAG SPACE DEBRIS BACK TO EARTH
By Hira Bashir, Latest Science News.
The full story: https://www.i4u.com/2018/03/127536/giant-harpoon-can-drag-space-debris-back-earth
Mar 18th, 2018

European aerospace company Airbus is developing a harpoon that can remove massive defunct satellites from space. An estimated 170 million pieces of space junk are orbiting around the Earth. Space junk is basically defunct satellites, fragments of rockets or other manmade objects that are no longer used and begin to float in low Earth orbit. The increasing amount of the debris orbiting around Earth could lead to catastrophic collisions with satellites and spacecrafts and can pose a threat to astronauts aboard them.

Space agencies around the world are trying different ways to remove this debris and to make space travel safer, but most of these efforts failed miserably. Now, engineers from Airbus UK have come up with a new plan. They are developing a giant harpoon that will drag space debris down into the Earth's atmosphere where it will burn up and disintegrate. The 1-meter long harpoon will be attached to a strong tether and pull junk out of orbit around Earth.

The elite's minions continually manipulate the moronic majority by prattling on about our "legacy" and "what we'll leave our children." If left to continue in our current state the only legacy we'll leave is extinction and mountains of trash. No matter where you go, even to the Moon, where we've left an estimated 500,000 pounds of trash to date, you'll find trash if people have been there. Ten years ago, I spent three months living on one of the most beautiful beaches on The Lost Coast of Northern California. Every Monday after the visit of the weekenders I picked up three large bags full of trash from the mile-long stretch of beach.

As we restore balance to our world we need to clean up and recycle the detritus of the elite's making that hasn't been repurposed. The previous articles are just some of the technologies being created and tried now. I have others that I think may be more efficient such as converting the unnecessary cargo ships' holds to receptacles for trash equipped with vacuum and shredding systems that will suck up massive amounts of ocean water strain the trash out of it, shred it and pump it into the holds while returning the water to the ocean. A fleet of ships equipped thusly could clean the oceans, even the microplastics, very quickly if we could perfect them.

As we power each home individually, we'll be abandoning the massive amounts of power production and transmission infrastructure that sterilize and pollute huge tracts of land. Tearing all that down and recycling it will provide us with billions of tons of materials and free up billions of acres for biological carbon sinks, populating, and simply enjoying the nature that will return as the scars heal.

Ridding the world of all the nuclear arms is a pet peeve of mine. To that end I suggest we figure out a way to round them all up, pack them into rockets and detonate them outside our solar system. That's just an extremely rough version of my idea. If we ever unite and change the paradigm, we can figure out how to accomplish a total denuclearization of the planet together.

IN THE END
YOU CAN'T FIX A PROBLEM BY BEING A PROBLEM.

"NEVER UNDERESTIMATE THE POWER OF STUPID PEOPLE IN LARGE GROUPS." – George Carlin

YOU HAVE TO BE A BETTER PERSON BEFORE YOU CAN HAVE A BETTER WORLD.

If you want a better world, stop marching around like helpless petulant children destroying everything in your path while shouting for the elite's minions to "do something" about the destruction they're abetting in, they don't answer to you and couldn't give a shit less about what you do or don't want and lip-service is all you're gonna get.

"YOU NEVER CHANGE THINGS BY FIGHTING THE EXISTING REALITY. TO CHANGE SOMETHING, BUILD A NEW MODEL THAT MAKES THE OLD MODEL OBSOLETE." – R. Buckminster Fuller

153

"THE SECRET OF CHANGE IS TO FOCUS ALL OF YOUR ENERGY, NOT ON FIGHTING THE OLD, BUT ON BUILDING THE NEW." – Socrates

Stop trying to fight violence with violence and your idiotically useless protesting, give up your ridiculously divisive beliefs and superstitions, and get educated. Take control of yourselves and your world and change it, stop expecting someone else whose only talent is lip-service to do it, especially the ones profiting from the destruction. I've given you a plan for reversing climate change and ending all the societal horrors the elite have created with a "Lamb's War" of unification, nullification, and paradigm restructuring, all you've gotta do is do it.

The saddest thing for me is knowing you won't because it's easier to remain stupid and irresponsible so you can blame greedy idiots for the damage you helped them do while you march around with your cardboard signs whining about what you don't want, destroying your property, and demanding things they have no intention of providing or doing. The second saddest thing is that you're so stupid you believe that's doing something productive.

However, in all fairness, you've come by those actions and beliefs honestly. You've been conditioned to think it works via positive and negative reinforcement conditioning for centuries.

A little food for thought: **the elite allow you to destroy property ("peacefully protest") because they make money when the property is rebuilt and new security measures are added. It also furthers their societal surveillance and oppression agendas.** If this wasn't the case you wouldn't have the "right" to do it.

"WE ARE NOT HERE CONCERNED WITH PEOPLE WHO PROFESS THE DEMOCRATIC FAITH BUT YEARN FOR THE DARK SECURITY OF DEPENDENCY WHERE THEY CAN BE SPARED THE BURDEN OF DECISIONS. RELUCTANT TO GROW UP, OR INCAPABLE OF DOING SO, THEY WANT TO REMAIN CHILDREN AND BE CARED FOR BY OTHERS. FOR THOSE WHO CAN, SHOULD BE ENCOURAGED TO GROW; FOR OTHERS THE FAULT LIES NOT IN THE SYSTEM BUT IN THEMSELVES." – Saul Alinsky, *Rules for Radicals*

"AS LONG AS YOU STILL EXPERIENCE THE STARS AS SOMETHING "ABOVE YOU" YOU LACK THE EYE OF KNOWLEDGE." – Friedrich Nietzsche, *Beyond Good and Evil*

"I THINK THE MOST MERCIFUL THING IN THE WORLD IS THE INABILITY OF THE HUMAN MIND TO CORRELATE ALL ITS CONTENTS. WE EXIST ON A PLACID ISLAND OF IGNORANCE. SURROUNDED BY THE BLACK SEAS OF INFINITY. AND IT WAS NOT MEANT THAT WE SHOULD VOYAGE FAR." – H. P. Lovecraft

IF YOU'RE EXPECTING A GOVERNMENT OR POLITICIAN TO MAKE THIS A BETTER WORLD, ALL YOU'RE GONNA GET IS A LOT OF LIES AND EMPTY PROMISES.

YOU CAN'T CHANGE ANYTHING UNTIL WE CHANGE EVERYTHING.

YOU CAN LEAD PEOPLE TO KNOWLEDGE BUT YOU CAN'T MAKE THEM THINK.

* 9 7 9 8 6 8 4 5 1 6 3 2 0 *